Balancing in the Balkans

RAYMOND TANTER
AND JOHN PSAROUTHAKIS

St. Martin's Press
New York

327.09
T16b

ISBN 0-312-21457-X

Library of Congress Cataloging-in-Publication Data
Tanter, Raymond.
    Balancing in the Balkans / Raymond Tanter and John
    Psarouthakis
        p. cm.
    Includes bibliographical references and index.
    ISBN 0-312-21457-X (cloth)
    1. Balkan Peninsula—Politics and government—1989– 2. Balkan
Peninsula—Foreign relations—1989– 3. National security—Balkan
Peninsula. 4. Yugoslav War, 1991–1995—Diplomatic history.
I. Psarouthakis, John, 1932– . II. Title.
DR48.6T36 1999
327'.09496'09049—dc21   98–52842
JK   CIP

First published: August, 1999

10 9 8 7 6 5 4 3 2 1

To the diplomats who beat swords into
plowshares in Bosnia and Kosovo—
Richard Holbrooke, Robert Gelbard,
and Christopher Hill—
and especially to their late colleagues—
Robert C. Frasure, Joseph
Kruzel, and S. Nelson Drew—
who perished prior to peace in Bosnia.

Central Balkan Region

Scale 1:3,550,000
Lambert Conformal Conic Projection,
standard parallels 40 N and 56 N

0   50 Kilometers
0   50 Miles

Serbia and Montenegro have asserted the formation of a joint
independent state, but this entity has not been formally
recognized as a state by the United States.

802567 (R02592) 6-96

Contents

ACKNOWLEDGMENTS

THANKS TO THE PAIDEIA FOUNDATION for financial assistance in the conduct of this entire research endeavor. Acknowledgments to Jeanne and Ernest Merlanti for providing financial assistance to Loretta Hieber. Joseph Gigliotti, Richard Kovacik, Anna Vania Song, and Elena Thomas were research assistants for the project. Jennifer Bucholz, Jacqueline DeLevie, Matthew Fogarty, Kristen Grauer, Aiman Mackie, Mona Motwani, and Suzanne Sukkar assisted in copyediting and indexing.

Thanks to Loretta Hieber; this book draws upon elite interviews she conducted in Belgrade, Bonn, London, Paris, Sarajevo, and Zagreb. In addition, the book draws upon United States Information Agency (USIA) focus group interviews and public opinion polls about Bosnia and Kosovo. Acknowledgments to Nancy Mendrala and Anna Sweeney of the USIA Office of Research and Media Reaction.

TWO SCHOOLS OF THOUGHT: GLOBALISM AND TRIBALISM

THIS BOOK BEGAN AS A DEBATE between the coauthors about how to achieve balance in the Balkans—how parties in Bosnia, Serbia, and Kosovo can learn moderation.[2] In the heartland of America, there is a race for the center because that is where the votes are; in the heartland of the Balkans, there is a race for the extremes because that is where the soul lies.

As the millennium approaches, there is crisis in Kosovo. Fighting once again rages in the Balkans. A Western air war against Serb military targets contrasts with a Serb ground war against ethnic Albanian civilians. Airstrikes from high-performance Western warplanes find their match in the low-technology Serb war machine as it ousts ethnic Albanians from Kosovo. NATO observes its fiftieth anniversary, and Western Europe dedicates its common currency. Both moves are indicative of a rising tide of globalism that sweeps the West. Meanwhile, Serbia memorializes the 600-year anniversary of its 1389 defeat in Kosovo at the hands of the Ottoman Turks, the predecessors of the ethnic Albanian Muslims. The Serb remembrance is characteristic of Belgrade's tendency to exacerbate ancient hatreds in order to mobilize the Serb population against ethnic minorities. Underlying the fighting and celebrations are two competing perspectives: globalism and tribalism.

Those who emphasize the divisive import of religion in the Balkan conflicts point to a change in the fault line between European states from the Cold War to the post–Cold War eras. For almost a half a century, the Iron Curtain was the dividing line between communist dictatorships and capitalist democracies in Europe. As the twenty-first century emerges, a new fault line separates Western Christians from Orthodox Christians and Muslims. The Balkans are again "Balkanized along religious lines."[3]

Despite the intense role of religious nationalism in the conflict among ethnic groups in Bosnia and Kosovo, coauthor Raymond Tanter tended to believe that secularist moderation might trump nationalist extremism. And thus, the Balkans might be Americanized. If so, the political moderation found in the midwestern United States might become a commodity exported to Bosnia and Kosovo.

But coauthor John Psarouthakis held that America is unique in time and place, and there is little market for its moderation in a world of parochial hatreds. Tanter believed that the quintessential American characteristic—balance—might be quickly exported to the Balkans. Psarouthakis thought that ethnic divisions would prevent the rapid adoption of American moderation. As the writing proceeded, both authors moved toward each other's positions, and thus to the center.

The first product of the authors' debate is a newspaper article on the deployment of American troops in Bosnia.[4] The issue of the article was whether the troops should return after the official withdrawal date. Tanter and Psarouthakis agreed that the troops should remain beyond the initial date of withdrawal, June 1998. Nevertheless, they approached the problem from two different perspectives defined, in part, by time.

The first school of thought has a fast time line. Tanter assumed that the time was ripe for interventionist forces to compel regional actors to negotiate an accord. The role of the outside forces was to provide security for opposing parties as they developed common economic and political bonds. This first school draws on the writing of diplomats and scholars like Richard Holbrooke, Warren Zimmermann, and Noel Malcolm.[5]

The second school has a slow time line. Psarouthakis presumed that outside forces needed time to achieve even a transitory, Pyrrhic victory—an ephemeral triumph achieved at excessive costs. External military forces can only compel regional parties in the short-term. Ethnic animosities prevent conflict resolution until the passage of time allows for a settlement. In other words, Psarouthakis recognized that dispute resolution might be possible when ethnic differences faded. The second school draws on such authors as Rebecca West and Robert Kaplan.[6]

Tanter drew upon deterrence, coercion, collective action, and globalization to make a case for the relevance of external forces to compel regional actors. Psarouthakis used ethnicity, religion, self-determination, and ancient hatreds to make an argument for the significance of internal factors as constraints on the effectiveness of outside intervention.

As the twenty-first century opens, there is a race between two ways of measuring time.[7] The first timepiece is the globalization clock. The second is the tribalization clock. At issue is the relative speed of these two timepieces—whether globalization is racing ahead of tribalization. Tanter believed that the rate of globalism is faster than the rate of tribalism. As an international entrepreneur, Psarouthakis is an advocate of globalization but sees globalism proceeding at different speeds according to location. When empires disintegrate, as took place in the former Soviet Union and Yugoslavia, tribalization abounds.

Globalization conjures up terms like integration, melting pot, and secular society. Also included in the concept of globalism are the new orthodoxy of the World Bank and the International Monetary Fund—economic restructuring agencies that advocate subsidy-slashing and privatization in the context of unhindered global capital flows.

Both authors believe that the United States aspires toward integration and that it is a nation in which different nationalities meld but have not melted into an American society. Not only is the United States a place where secularism triumphs over religious extremism, it is also a source of global capital. Consequently, the American private sector can provide financial incentives for subnational groups in

Bosnia and Kosovo. The hope is that ancient hatreds might decline with the growth of common economic and political institutions.

As an advocate of racial integration, Psarouthakis nevertheless believed that it takes time to rid the world of segregationists and ethnic cleansers. He saw the rise of sacred societies as impediments to the march toward global secularism. It took time for South Africa's apartheid regime to fall. Similarly, it will take time to rid the former Yugoslavia of ethnic cleansing. Meanwhile, sacred states will continue to grow from the ashes of disintegrating empires.

Both Tanter and Psarouthakis see America as a nation-state, while they view entities like Iran as sacred-states. They believe that neither the nation-state nor the sacred-state will be the prevailing authority in the future. Rather, there is a move toward a borderless, Internet-based, global electronic village. Here, politics will be less important than information and entertainment. At issue between the authors is time. Tanter's optimistic forecast occurs sooner than later, while Psarouthakis' time line stretches farther into the future.

Regarding entertainment, globalization involves American exports that help transform the world and imports to the United States that accelerate cultural change in that country. Exports to the global village include the M&Ns: The "M's" consist of Macintosh, Microsoft, McDonalds, MTV, and Major League Baseball. The "N's" are the National Football League, National Basketball Association, and National Hockey League—NFL, NBA, and NHL.

It is not only tall Croatians who admire the "imported" Croatian basketball player Toni Kukoc of the Chicago Bulls. With respect to Major League Baseball, consider the New York Yankees, Florida Marlins, and the Los Angeles Dodgers: players imported from Latin American comprise about 25 percent of their rosters.

When the "Russian five"—Konstantinov, Larinov, Fetisov, Koslov, and Federov—skated as a line, they were not in Moscow but in fact were skating for the Detroit Red Wings. When the Red Wings visited the White House after winning the Stanley Cup, captain Steve Yzerman remarked that his teammates included Russians, Swedes, Canadians, and, "Oh yes, I think there's an American!" Three of the Russian five brought the Stanley Cup to Moscow as a supreme American-Canadian "export."

It is a quite a stretch to imagine that parties in conflict in the Balkans who pay attention to American sports are less likely to fight each other. But along with such entertainment icons come American soldiers, diplomats, and economic advisers. The cultural, political/ military, and economic vectors line up to promote U.S. influence abroad. Tanter believed that the "M&N" cultural exports have had a rapid impact on Americanizing the world. He assumed that the cultural icons reinforce Washington's political-military global clout and buttress American diplomacy from the Balkans, to Baghdad, to Beijing.

While Psarouthakis celebrated the export of American entertainment icons, he believed that the Balkanization of borders, the Lebanonization of lands, and the Somalism of societies rather than Americanization dominated the post–Cold War era.[8] Born in Europe and bred in America, Psarouthakis worried about nations within states. He pointed to the case of Kosovo. Over 90 percent of the population of Kosovo is ethnic Albanian, but Kosovo is a troubled nation within another state, Serbia. When nations exist within states and there is a difference between the ethnic identities of the nation and the state, Psarouthakis believed that this contrast is a recipe for political instability.

Tanter acknowledged that nations within states might give rise to ethnic conflict, but he cautioned that ethnicity is not destiny. Both authors believe that corrupt politicians exacerbate ethnic tensions for selfish political purposes at the expense of the national interest. Expanding economic ties among ethnic groups allow for the growth of common political institutions. On top of local and regional collective economic action, globalization offers nations within states an occasion to rise above ethnic conflicts.

Time, again, is the core of the dispute between the authors. Tanter's clock sped along under the assumption that external forces can deter, coerce, and build collective regional institutions. The velocity of the Psarouthakis timepiece reflects the constraints of ethnicity, nationalism, and religion. Also at issue initially between the authors was whether the very existence of the Balkans within the global village was sufficient to facilitate the growth of economic ties and political institutions that bind the parties into an interdependent entity.

Despite their differing answers, they agree that the United States-led coalition needs to remain engaged in the Balkans. The West must maintain a preponderance of military power throughout the region. It should be prepared to use military force and to provide military and economic incentives to the villagers along border areas among Albania, the Kosovo province of Serbia, and Macedonia.

CIRCUMSTANCE AND CHOICE

Underlying the Tanter-Psarouthakis debate is the issue of how to explain events in Yugoslavia. At the beginning of the debate, Psarouthakis explained such events as primarily a result of historical and psychological circumstance. Tanter interpreted these occurrences as mainly due to rational choice. When analysts focus on either circumstance or choice they miss the whole picture. Both need to be taken into account in explaining outcomes in the Balkans.

On one hand, circumstance designates an approach that makes Freudian-like assumptions. Politicians are victims of their historical environment; circumstance explains their behavior. Leaders attribute their own violent behavior to a hostile milieu that leaves them little choice. Such politicians explain their own behavior as a result of circumstance: "We Serbs had no choice but to kill the Muslims in Bosnia." And from the perspective of Greater Serbia, Serbs explain Bosnian Muslim behavior as a result of choice: "The Bosnian Muslims are simply evil, and thus they choose to fight our Serb brethren in our land." According to the behavior resulting from circumstance explanation, leaders pursue risky behavior in order to avoid losses determined by others. And, because they pay more attention to losses than gains, these leaders are not easily deterred or coerced.

On the other hand, choice represents an approach that makes Machiavellian-like rational assumptions. In this paradigm, politicians manipulate people in order to gain strategic advantage. Leaders choose options because the expected gains exceed the anticipated losses. To deter or coerce them, leaders can make credible threats that raise expected costs to a level that is higher than anticipated benefits.

After performing the research for this book, the authors take a balanced approach. They assume that both circumstance and choice are complementary explanations of outcomes in the Balkans. Although Milosevic is a politician who uses ethnicity as a lever for political gain, ethnic animosities also constrain his freedom of action. In other words, politicians do not create ethnic animosities, although they often exacerbate these divisions. If it were not for preexisting ethnic hatreds, the Milosevics of the world would not be able to manipulate these differences for political advantage.

The hope is that balance between the authors regarding globalism and tribalism or circumstance and choice will compliment a balance among the antagonists in the Balkans. If so, Bosnia and Kosovo might experience the effects of globalization that have transformed states like Hungary and Poland from socialist command economies to capitalist market-oriented economies. But before a nation can enter the global economy, it needs to transition from war to peace. Just as Hungary and Poland moved from Cold War to warm peace as members of the Atlantic Alliance, Serbia, Bosnia, and Kosovo may move from hot war to cold peace.

CRISIS IN KOSOVO

Consider objectives, options, scenarios, and outcomes regarding the crisis in Kosovo. Objectives are the goals that decisionmakers prefer, options are the choices available to them, scenarios are the potential events not under their control that constrain their alternatives, and outcomes are the results of choices under constraints.

Objectives

NATO objectives in Kosovo concern destruction, removal, repatriation, and protection. The first aim is to destroy enough of the Serb military forces so that Belgrade is not a threat to ethnic Albanians or to neighboring countries. The second goal is to remove most of the Serb military and paramilitary units from Kosovo. The third purpose is to repatriate ethnic-Albanian refugees back to Kosovo, and the fourth aim is to create an international military protection force, with NATO at its core.

A disconnect exists among the four objectives. Destruction and removal of Serb forces fit together as the means by which NATO would like to effect the combined goals of repatriation and protection of ethnic Albanians. Achievement of destruction and removal, however, does not automatically yield repatriation and protection. The link between the first and second pairs of objectives could emerge from informal tacit bargaining, a ceasefire followed by formal negotiations, or an imposed settlement ratified at a peace conference after a decisive victory in an air/land battle. Such negotiations would also determine the final outcome for the leadership of Yugoslavia.

Options

In light of the NATO objectives, consider political and military options facing the alliance. Political options include reconciliation, containment, and regime change; military options consist of airstrikes or a combination of air war and ground combat.

Reconciliation is a policy that assumes adherence of an adversary to external demands. Containment is a strategy of imposing punishments, such as economic sanctions and periodic use of force in order to compel a degree of compliance. Regime change is a policy using brute force rather than rewards or threats to displace the leadership, for example, overthrowing the government or imposing a new political system on the country.

With regard to the military options, only airstrikes with ground combat can bring about a comprehensive NATO success. An air campaign alone would fall short of achieving victory for NATO.

Scenarios and Outcomes

The likelihood of each outcome depends on the scenario that unfolds, which in turn follows from the option chosen. Consider these scenarios: Serb triumph; standoff, but Serbs dominate; deadlock; stalemate, but NATO dominates; NATO victory.

Following each scenario are outcomes involving the status of Kosovo and concerning the leadership of Yugoslavia.

Outcomes for Status of Kosovo. The possible outcomes for Kosovo are puppet province, partition, Rambouillet, Rambouillet Minus, and Rambouillet Plus. (Rambouillet is a village near Paris that was the site of negotiations during February 1999.) These outcomes range from least to most favorable for the NATO allies.

One result earmarks Kosovo as a puppet province under Serb sovereignty. This approach accepts the Serb depopulation of ethnic Albanians in Kosovo, assumes the presence of large numbers of Serb military and paramilitary forces in that province, and precludes international military protection for Kosovo.

Another outcome—partition—divides Kosovo into Serb and ethnic-Albanian areas. Were this partition based on geographical proximity, Eastern Orthodox Christian religious sites and mineral deposits important to Serbia would pose a problem. Because these sites are scattered throughout Kosovo, negotiated geographical partition is a diplomatic nonstarter. Geographical partition would be feasible only if imposed by NATO as victor in combat against Serbia. Under a negotiated settlement favoring the Serbs, partition might take the form of a polka-dot pattern. It would be difficult, however, for an international military force to provide security to ethnic Albanians if Belgrade controlled sites and deposits within densely populated ethnic-Albanian areas.

In contrast to the polka-dot version of partition, division based on geographical proximity would place repatriated refugees in the ethnic-Albanian portion in the southeast and southwest of Kosovo. Ethnic Albanians would rename this area Kosova. The Serbs would occupy the partitioned entity of the northeast and northwest, which would retain the name of Kosovo. With respect to the ethnic-Albanian portion, Serbia and Macedonia fear that Kosova might unite with Albania to create Greater Albania. This potential unit is a threat to current states in the region because it attracts ethnic Albanians from other parts of the Balkans.

A further outcome, though unlikely after the spring 1999 hostilities, is the Rambouillet proposal that emerged from the February negotiations. This approach includes substantial autonomy for ethnic Albanians, withdrawal of most Serb forces from Kosovo, disarmament of the Kosovo Liberation Army (KLA), and a referendum within three years for ethnic Albanians to vote on independence. At Rambouillet, the major powers and the Kosovars agreed on the terms, but Belgrade declined to consent. An ensuing diplomatic stalemate prompted NATO airstrikes, and Serbia accelerated its efforts to expel ethnic Albanians from Kosovo.

An additional outcome is Rambouillet Minus, which decreases diplomatic gains ethnic Albanians achieved in the original Rambouillet proposal. This approach is a minus because it reduces the degree of Kosovar autonomy, diminishes the number of KLA troops in Kosovo, lessens the size and role of a NATO military protection force, and increases the number of Serb troops to be deployed in Kosovo.

A final outcome is Rambouillet Plus, which builds on the initial Rambouillet proposal and extends the diplomatic gains of the ethnic Albanians. This outcome goes beyond mere autonomy for the ethnic Albanians and sets up a framework to facilitate independence for them. In addition, Rambouillet Plus proposes a provision to allow the will of the people to be expressed and for ethnic Albanians to vote on independence not in three years but within a shorter period of time, such as a year. Rambouillet Plus requires withdrawal of all Serb forces from Kosovo, forgoes disarmament of the Kosovo Liberation Army (KLA), and creates a newly formed Republic of Kosova as a NATO protectorate. In order to make this outcome acceptable to Belgrade, however, there might have to be a compromise that would give Serbs access to certain religious sites without giving Belgrade sovereignty over these areas.

Because every war must end, at issue is the balance of power or preponderance of power among former combatants when combat ceases. If Serbia emerges as undisputed victor and the Brussels-based NATO needs political cover for an exit, then the puppet province result is conceivable. If there is a comparative standoff between Belgrade and Brussels, then partition becomes viable. On one hand, if neither side is a clear winner but Belgrade is in the most favorable political/military position, Rambouillet Minus is a conse-

quence that comes to mind. On the other hand, if the result of fighting is too close to call but the allies are in the most advantageous
diplomatic and military position, then Rambouillet Plus is an outcome that surfaces.

Also worthy of discussion is the original Rambouillet proposal,
which assumes a permissive security environment—a situation in
which military forces enter a region with the permission of the parties to help implement an agreement among them. A non-permissive
environment is one in which military forces fight their way into a region. In the context of the benign situation, a NATO military protection force would provide security for ethnic Albanians, and
Kosovo would resume its autonomous status under Serb sovereignty. However, the original Rambouillet proposal is defunct due to
the escalation of fighting during the spring of 1999.

Outcomes for the Leadership of Yugoslavia. The set of outcomes
pertaining to the leadership of Yugoslavia are that Milosevic retains
power on his own terms, that he remains in Belgrade on NATO's
terms, that he is ousted by a coup, or that he leaves office in a peaceful, democratic transition. The outcome in this regard would emerge
from informal tacit bargaining, a ceasefire followed by formal negotiations, or an imposed settlement ratified at a peace conference
following decisive NATO victory.

Tacit bargaining and/or formal negotiations might yield a compromise settlement. Milosevic retains power, NATO ceases its air
war, ethnic Albanians return to their homes, and NATO provides
the core of an international protection force, similar to Rambouillet. This accord is a compromise in that NATO achieves repatriation
and protection for the ethnic Albanians and Milosevic retains power
and obtains an end to the air war.

In the event that NATO combines ground and air forces and
defeats Serbia, either military coup or democratic transition is a
possible outcome. Serbia's defeat might precipitate a coup d'etat,
which is unlikely because leaders generally gain strength when their
nations are under attack. More likely, however, is for Milosevic to
be replaced during a democratic transition following an imposed
settlement.

After World War II, defeated Nazi Germany and Imperial Japan became democracies in which an elected leadership replaced prewar rulers. Similarly, following NATO's war over Kosovo, the allies may impose a democratic order on a defeated Serbia, and an elected leadership would come to power untainted by internal repression, hostilities, and war crimes.

In the spring 1999 hostilities, NATO considered the following strategies: compromising its aims and entering into a ceasefire, retaining the goals of destruction, removal, repatriation, and protection while intensifying the air war, or broadening the objectives to include overthrow of Milosevic in a combined air/land battle.

Compromise consists of striking a deal with Milosevic. It might include merely degrading rather than destroying Serb forces, evicting some but not all Serb forces from Kosovo, repatriating civilian ethnic-Albanian refugees while restricting the Kosovo military arm—the KLA, and reducing the role of NATO in the international military protection force for Kosovo.

Scenarios emerging from the spring 1999 hostilities include victory, defeat, and stalemate, as previously discussed. Victory for NATO means achieving the objectives of destruction, removal, repatriation, and protection. If NATO wins outright, moreover, overthrow could be enacted through imposition of democracy or precipitation of a coup d'etat by opposition forces within Serbia. If the Serbs triumph, Belgrade could implement the puppet-province outcome. If neither side emerges as a clear winner but NATO holds the balance of power, then the allies could realize Rambouillet Plus. If there is no clear victor but the balance of power tilts toward the Serbs, and then Belgrade can effect Rambouillet Minus. Finally, if there is utter stalemate, the unpalatable outcome of partition becomes probable.

Under the assumption that the Serbs win and the puppet-province outcome occurs, ancient hatreds, tribalization, and ethnic cleansing would be vindicated. Ethnic, nationalistic, and religious differences would be emphasized over common cultural, international, and secular similarities within the Balkans.

Assuming the allies win and at least Rambouillet Plus is the outcome, NATO could create an environment that allows for collective economic action and the construction of common political institutions throughout the Balkans. Rather than the destabilizing creation of Greater Albania, Rambouillet Plus might yield a stable economic federation among the neighboring entities, which consist of Albania, Bosnia, Kosova, Macedonia, as well as Serbia and Montenegro. If this federation established a preferential trading relationship with the European Union within the constraints of the World Trade Organization, the tribalization and ancient hatreds of the past might yield globalization and economic prosperity in the future. There would be a transition from combat to cooperation through commerce.

CHAPTER ONE

COMBAT, COERCION, AND COOPERATION

CONSIDER THE BALKANS AS A LABORATORY for exploring ideas about
globalism and tribalism as well as about circumstance and choice.
The application of Western diplomacy and force to the regional
warfare in the Balkans offers an opportunity to test propositions
about how to overcome ethnicity in the race for peace and security.

Absent the Cold War, Western diplomacy in the Balkans is like
a dance among quarreling friends. This dance of the diplomats allows Balkan politicians freedom of action. While the friends feud,
local foes are free to bolster their domestic political fortunes by exacerbating ethnic tensions. Lacking the political and economic intervention of outside parties, regional politicians play the ethnic
card with ease. By initiating short-term coercive diplomacy and mid-
term economic action, interventionists may be able to further long-
term political cooperation in the Balkans.

During a December 1997 speech to American soldiers in Bosnia,
President Bill Clinton acknowledged the coercive role played by external forces in the Balkans: "Without [American soldiers], the warring parties would never have disengaged." But during his address
in Sarajevo to the Bosnians, Clinton downplayed the coercive role
of external forces. Rather, he emphasized the need for the parties
themselves to rise above ethnicity to find a basis for cooperation.
Clinton said to a group of Bosnian Croats, Muslims, and Serbs:

"The future is up to you—not the Americans, not the Europeans, not to anyone else."[1] While the threat of military engagement was the basis for coercion, the promise of commerce among the parties might be a basis of cooperation. The effectiveness of threats or promises might be examined through the tumultuous events in the Balkans.

WHY AND WHITHER DAYTON?[2]

The Dayton Accords of 1995 began to close a chapter of the warfare among Bosnian Muslims, Bosnian Serbs, and Croats. An assumption of the accords was that coercive diplomacy would encourage conflict resolution in Bosnia, and that outcome would facilitate the settlement of disputes in adjoining areas. Although the Dayton agreement helped to bring the Bosnian war to a close, a nearby conflict between Serbia and Kosovo escalated. Successful resolution of one conflict does not guarantee peace throughout the region. So as the 1990s closed, fighting in Kosovo threatened a fragile ceasefire in Bosnia. The diplomats at Dayton danced around the problem of Kosovo because the Serbian delegation declined to expand the mandate for Dayton to include what it considered a purely internal matter. As a result, the Serbian regime in Belgrade planted the seeds for conflict escalation and expansion rather than cooperation and commerce.

A main thread of the analysis regarding coercion is that, in the context of a credible preponderance of external power, coercive diplomacy creates an opportunity to bring local warring actors to the table. And, if there were a balance of power among the local parties, diplomatic persuasion by external actors has a chance of gaining the compliance of the antagonists for a lasting peace.

With respect to short-term coercion, at issue is what made the parties come to the negotiating table and consent to the Dayton Peace Agreement. On November 22, 1995, the presidents of Bosnia, Croatia, and Serbia, on behalf of the Bosnia Serb Republic, initialed the Dayton Peace Agreement. The formal signing occurred in Paris on December 14, 1995. The accords among the republics of the former Yu-

goslavia impose a ceasefire, authorize military and civilian implementation programs, and aim to establish a central government of Bosnia.

With respect to mid-term cooperation, what will it take to implement the accords and maintain the peace? Dayton occurred as result of a preponderance of NATO military power and the
application of multilateral economic sanctions. Whether Dayton
evolves depends not only on military capabilities and sanctions but
also on developments in nearby Kosovo. In the context of dual
ceasefires in Bosnia and Kosovo, there is a chance to create economic ties and common political institutions among the ethnic
groups. Power and commerce acting together might help realize a
peace scenario.

In order to set the scene for considering the "why" and
"whither" Dayton questions, here is a discussion of levels of analysis, balance-of-power and preponderance-of-power principles, as
well as historical developments in the former Yugoslavia. In addition, there is a treatment of ethnic conflicts and interventionist solutions and a consideration of the partition of Bosnia along ethnic
lines. Finally, this study addresses scenarios for the future and policy
options in the present for both Bosnia and Kosovo. In addition to
knowing how to bring about a balance of power in Bosnia, it is in-
structive to understand who came to the table.[3]

POLITICS OF PERSONALITY

The politics of personality school of thought contrasts sharply with
the classical deterrence and coercive diplomacy literature. The classical school places personality in a "black box." It is necessary only
to assume that individuals will act rationally in pursuit of their
goals. It is not necessary to look within the black box to discover the
personality attributes of the decisionmakers. However, personality
is relevant if leaders are risk averse in pursuit of national objectives
and risk acceptant in avoiding losses. In the first instance, they are
subject to strategies like deterrence and coercive diplomacy; in the
latter, they are less subject to such strategies.[4] In either case, there is
a need to discover the risk propensity of a leadership.

One reason for personalizing conflicts is because the motivations of leaders might explain their risk-taking propensity. In this regard, there is a body of literature that seeks to explain politics on the basis of psychology.[5] This approach focuses on personality attributes of involved leaders rather than such impersonal factors as regional and international system attributes. The balance of power among opposing parties, moreover, illustrates a systemic characteristic.

During the Cold War, America's enemies of the hour were the likes of Stalin, Khrushchev, and Brezhnev. With the breakup of the Soviet empire, new adversaries burst onto the international scene. They included American-defined international outlaws, such as Ayatollah Khomeni of Iran, Muammar Qadhafi of Libya, and Kim Jong-Il of North Korea. They were the new demons of the day, but they were not the only bad guys in town. The Bosnian conflict introduced new devils to the rogues' gallery: Slobodan Milosevic, Radovan Karadzic, and General Ratko Mladic.

Throughout much of the 1990s, the press abounded with stories about the outrageous conduct of these latest rogue leaders and their followers. In June 1996, the International Criminal Tribunal for the former Yugoslavia in The Hague issued indictments for the arrest of eight men. The tribunal charged them with sexual assault for the purpose of torture and enslavement. United Nations investigators believed these individuals were ultimately responsible for the systematic rapes perpetrated by Bosnian Serb soldiers and paramilitaries. In effect, the accusation was that sexual assault was an established part of ethnic cleansing.

A year later, NATO-led peacekeeping troops seized one Bosnian Serb suspected of war crimes and killed another in a shoot-out in northwestern Bosnia. This military action was the first attempt by NATO to arrest any of the dozens of suspects at large. During May 1997, the International Criminal Tribunal found one of the most notorious of these suspects—Dusko Tadic—guilty on 11 of 34 charges leveled against him.[6]

From the point of view of the "behavior as circumstance" school, it is difficult to pin responsibility on individuals for behavior that derives from a history of hatred. From the perspective of the rational choice school, criminal behavior like ethnic cleansing is a consciously chosen policy deserving of retribution.

The process of arresting those indicted of war crimes indicates that the balance of power within Bosnia is in transition. As power shifts from ethnic-cleansers to nation-builders, the dream of a multi-ethnic Bosnian federation comes into view. But if the holders of the balance fail to combine force with diplomacy, this dream is liable to turn into a nightmare of tragic proportions.

The indictments of war criminals and military operations to arrest them illustrate the process by which the international community blames individuals for war atrocities. Holding people responsible makes sense because the criminal justice system cannot convict impersonal factors. Even though the lack of a balance of power may contribute to the outbreak of war, only individuals can be indicted and found guilty for their misbehavior.

Because of their misdeeds, it is possible to justify the censure of leaders like Milosevic, Karadzic, and Mladic, but one should not overlook factors at a different level of analysis than the individual level. That is, people operate within the constraints of system level attributes. Two such attributes are a balance of power and a preponderance of power. In particular, whether there is a balance or a preponderance of power is critical in explaining why individuals eventually comply with international demands to negotiate a ceasefire. These regional and international system conditions may be as significant as personality factors in explaining why the parties came to the table in order to negotiate a ceasefire in the Balkans.

In addition to personality and international system-level factors, there are local conditions that account for whether actors will make a lasting peace. Foremost among these are their commitment to collective economic action and the balance of power among ethnic groups. Prior to building common institutions there has to be a certain degree of stability among the parties. Indeed, external actors have issued many demands for the regional parties in the Balkans to cease fighting.

BALANCING PRINCIPLES AND COMPLIANCE

Compliance involves conflict prevention and conflict resolution. From a rational choice perspective, deterrence is a tool for the prevention of conflict, and coercion is a device for the resolution of conflict, albeit in favor of the coercer rather than on mutual terms. At issue is what it takes to deter and coerce.

This issue can be examined by answering two questions: Prior to the occurrence of war during 1991, would threats of economic sanctions and military force have prevented the outbreak of fighting? And once war occurred, would threats or actual sanctions and force coerce the parties to accept a ceasefire? To answer these two questions, it would be helpful to make rational calculations about three balances: power, resolve, and interests.

Balance-of-power theorists suggest that equilibrium of military capabilities among the parties is one reason for the success of deterrence. Indeed, the concept of balance of power nests within the idea of general deterrence.[7] One aim of a balance-of-power system is to manage power in a pluralistic world of independent actors. The threat that an opposing coalition might intervene constrains potential disturbers of the peace.

The balancer is a key concept in the international relations literature. A balancer is a nation that remains detached from the rivalries of other actors until the time is ripe for action. Its interests are best served by the maintenance of a global or regional balance of power until there is a challenge to that balance. As long as the other nations are in equilibrium, the balancer need not intervene. If one side gains enough strength to tip the scales, however, the balancer may have to take action. It can join the weaker side and bring the scales back into symmetry or join the stronger coalition and tip the scales even more.

From the time of the breakup of Yugoslavia until the Dayton Accords, Serbia had been the dominant military power in the region. But Belgrade did not function as holder of the balance because it did not act to tip scales in a disinterested way. Rather, Belgrade tilted toward the Bosnian Serbs because of its desire to recreate a Greater Serbia. In this fashion, Serbia simply sought to dominate the other former republics of Yugoslavia.

When Belgrade complied with American initiatives at Dayton, the accords changed the balance at both the system and regional levels. NATO became the holder of the overall balance. As such,

NATO tended to side with the weaker parties (Bosnian Muslims and Croats) against the stronger side (Serbia and Bosnian Serbs). In the post-Dayton era, the issue arises of how peace among the parties will be maintained. The thesis of this study is that a balance of power among ethnic groups coupled with their commitment to common economic action is a way to preserve the gains of Dayton. Like the balance of power, the concept of a preponderance of power also derives from the idea of general deterrence. The literature finding that preponderance of power successfully deters and coerces includes several essays and studies.[8]

One purpose of dominant power is to deter a challenger from ever defying the wishes of the status quo powers in the first place: a balance-of-power system rests on the assumption that the challenger would be deterred after venturing to test the system; and a preponderance-of-power system assumes that the challenger would not act because of the prospect of overwhelming power arrayed against it. Both the balance-of-power and preponderance systems presuppose that deterrence and coercion would be a consequence of relative military capabilities of the opposing coalitions.

With respect to the Balkans, the potential of NATO to become holder of the balance and the possible predominance of its military capabilities were never in doubt among the parties in conflict. In question, however, was the willingness among the NATO members to act as a collective security organization and follow through on its threats. In other words, the regional parties discounted NATO credibility, interests, and solidarity. Indeed, there is an international relations literature that downplays the role of military capabilities in deterrence and coercion.[9] Rather, balance of resolve and balance of interests as well as the exposure of an actor's civilian population to attack may be more important than relative capabilities among the parties.

Resolve concerns an imbalance in the determination of the parties: the actor with the greater resolve can coerce the one with less conviction. Interests involve an imbalance of stakes: the party that has more to gain can coerce the actor with less at stake. Vulnerability of population pertains to an imbalance of civilian exposure to attack: the party with the least exposure to attack is in a position to coerce the actor with the most vulnerable population.[10]

The main regional actors in the Balkan tragedy—the Bosnian Croats, Muslims, and Serbs; the ethnic Albanians in the Serbian province of Kosovo; the government of Croatia; and the government of Serbia—had a definite imbalance of resolve and interest in their favor in comparison with external parties. It was only after the commitment of Britain and France to serve as peacekeepers on the ground as well as the engagement of NATO's prestige and airpower that the perceived stakes and interests began to change in the direction of the allies. Hence, their military capabilities were not salient in effecting compliance among the ethnic groups until the balance of resolve and interests tilted in favor of the interventionists.

In connection with vulnerability of civilian populations, there was a relative imbalance among the ethnic groups. The Bosnian Muslims were the most vulnerable and hence most likely to be coercible by their enemies. Despite civilian exposure to rape, pillage, and shelling from the Bosnian Serbs, however, the Bosnian Muslims were just as steadfast as the other groups. Similarly, Muslims in Kosovo were as vulnerable to Serbs from Belgrade as the Bosnian Muslims were to the Bosnian Serbs. Yet, the Kosovars also refused to comply with the demands of the Serbs. Despite being outgunned, Muslims in both Bosnia and Kosovo were not coercible.

Two schools of thought seek to explain why the Bosnian Muslim regime in Sarajevo and the Kosovars in Pristina held out against the Serbs when their respective civilian populations were exposed to great dangers. One approach uses rational choice assumptions, and the other employs prospect theory. Rational choice assumes that actors engage in a cost-benefit analysis to maximize expected gains. Consequently, if coercers make credible threats that instill fear, the targets of the coercion should comply. The expected gains from compliance should be greater than the expected losses from noncompliance. Conversely, if the targets do not comply, it is because the threats were not credible and did not raise the anticipated costs higher than the foreseen gains.

According to rational choice theory, Sarajevo decided to risk civilian casualties for the benefit it expected to derive from continuing to fight the Bosnian Serbs. The Bosnian Muslim leadership seemed to value the long-term goal of self-determination of a sovereign multiethnic state over the short-term safety of its civilian population. The foreseen gain of noncompliance, self-determination, outweighed the anticipated losses from Bosnian Serbian attacks against the Muslim population. Likewise, from a rational choice viewpoint, ethnic Albanians in Pristina Kosovo also risked civilian casualties for the expected value of achieving independence from Belgrade. Again, Muslims desired the goal of self-determination more than they feared the loss of civilian security.

Building upon rational choice, a second approach is prospect theory. If actors frame a situation in terms of gains, they should act in accordance with rational choice prescription: compliance when the risk exceeds the expected gains. And, if parties frame the situation in terms of losses, they tend to accept high risks to avoid those losses. Hence, actors might accept the risks of noncompliance in order to avert potential losses, irrespective of the potential gains of compliance. The Muslims of Sarajevo may have framed their war with Bosnian Serbs as a potential danger to the newly acquired sovereignty over the whole of Bosnia. If so, prospect theory anticipates that the Bosnian Muslims would risk civilian casualties to avoid a loss of sovereignty.

BALANCING THROUGH HISTORY

Consider a discussion of balancing through history in order to set the scene for a treatment of policy outcomes in light of future scenarios in Chapter Seven. Any discussion of balancing principles should take into account the geopolitical situation of the Balkans, in particular, Kosovo in relation to Bosnia. Whichever group held Kosovo had considerable strategic advantage in that they might control entry to Bosnia and have access to northern Albania. In addition, this group could threaten to cut the link between Serbia and the Macedonian-Aegean region.[11]

From ancient to modern history, the Balkans have overflowed with examples concerning the relevance of balancing ideas for conflict prevention and resolution. In ancient Greece, there was a precedent for the successful pursuit of balance-of-power policies.

Thucydides, in his account of the Peloponnesian War, wrote that both Corcyra (Corfu) and Corinth petitioned Athens for help. Athens sided with the Corcyreans on balance-of-power grounds. As holder of the balance, Athens was unwilling to see a naval power of such magnitude as Corcyra sacrificed to Corinth, though they could weaken each other by mutual conflict. As Athens might eventually have to wage war with the fleets of Corinth, an alliance with Corcyra, the greatest naval power of the region, was advantageous.

A modern illustration of a successful balance-of-power system involves Russia and Serbia. In the 1870s, Moscow deployed over one thousand volunteers to fight in the Serbian army against the Turks. In spite of objections from much of Europe as well as economic difficulties in Russia, Moscow succeeded in defending the territorial integrity of its Slavic kin in Serbia against the military forces of the Ottoman Empire. Moscow was able to intervene in a limited war for finite purposes; a general war did not occur.

At the beginning of the twentieth century, great power intervention in the Balkans was minimal. Consequently, the Balkan Wars of 1912 (Bulgaria, Serbia, and Greece versus the Ottoman Empire) and 1913 (Bulgaria versus Greece, Serbia, Romania, and the Ottoman Empire) did not spread. Even though Serbia doubled its territory and increased its population by about half during these regional wars, there was no general conflagration that engulfed the whole of Europe. But when a Serbian assassin killed Austrian Archduke Franz-Ferdinand on June 28, 1914, Vienna declared war on Serbia. Subsequent Great Power intervention prevented the normal operation of the balance of power. This sequence of events illustrates a failed balance-of-power system.

Prior to the outbreak of World War I, Moscow stood behind Belgrade. Instead of confronting a major Serbian defeat in the Balkans, Moscow reluctantly agreed to intervene on behalf of Belgrade. In doing so, Russia disrupted the regional balance of power in the Balkans. Had Russia not stood with Serbia, the regional balance might have been able to sustain the peace. In the absence of a preponderance of military capabilities by any one of the Great Powers, there was an unstable balance that could not maintain peace in the region.

The failure of the balance of power to maintain the peace was an issue in World War I. The inadequacy of balancing mechanisms resulted in mutual misperceptions followed by escalation through miscalculation. Because of a fear of being left behind in a race for security, mutual insecurity was the outcome. There was a perceptual security dilemma.[12] A perceptual security dilemma occurs when decisionmakers overrate the advantages of taking the offensive or the hostility of others. The parties were unable to anticipate the consequences of their efforts to reinforce deterrence and to coerce one another.

The disruption of the balance of power provided an incentive for escalation. After Russia tipped the balance, Serbia not only had the military capability to attack, but it had a strategic interest to do so. The incentives for attack outweighed any military risk Turkey might have posed. Serbia jumped through a window of opportunity opened by Russia.

The two World Wars share similarities but also have differences. With respect to similarities, the processes that began the two wars involved threat perception. Misperception of threat can produce an overestimation or underestimation of danger. Prior to World War I, actors overestimated threats. Prior to World War II, they underestimated threats. An unintended spiraling of events characterized the First World War.

A failure to deter characterized the Second World War. During 1939, a dominant alliance failed to coalesce in order to deter Nazi aggression. Rather than the runaway escalation of hostility experienced in 1914, a failure to deter and coerce set the scene for Nazi aggression against its neighbors. World War II began when Nazi Germany took over Poland, Czechoslovakia, and Yugoslavia. By either force of arms or coercion, Berlin took over central Europe. A blocking coalition formed too late for successful deterrence.

The failure of a balancing mechanism to operate because of mutual misperceptions had different characteristics in World Wars I and II. In World War II, Britain and France were not afraid of escalation via miscalculation. Rather, they were engaged in wishful thinking that appeasement would satisfy Hitler, and thus there would not be a need to reinforce deterrence. Rather than reinforcement of deterrence that provoked war in the case of 1914, there was a failure to deter Nazi Germany that permitted war in 1939. An unintended war occurred in 1914 because the parties misjudged the effects of their alignments in freezing the balance of power. A war occurred in 1939 because the parties misjudged the consequences of their appeasement policy, which failed to prevent Nazi Germany from using its preponderance of power against smaller states.

For one small state in southern Europe, Yugoslavia, failure to deter Hitler in 1939 caused a disaster two years later. This failure paved the way for future hostilities in the Balkans. Nazi Germany forced the Yugoslav army to surrender on April 17, 1941. Germany and Italy, the Axis powers, dismembered Yugoslavia. Nazi allies in Croatia, the Ustasa regime, killed Serbs, Jews, and Gypsies in great numbers. The absence of a preponderance of power by an opposing coalition in the 1940s left Hitler alone on the world stage to play out the World War II tragedy. The curtain only fell when an ascendant coalition led by Moscow and Washington emerged in victory. The World War II destruction of Yugoslavia was a consequence of external forces. The post–Cold War breakup of that country was a result of internal implosion.

In addition to the overwhelming imbalance in military capability in Germany's favor, there also was an imbalance of resolve and interests. Hitler's stronger determination gave him a tremendous advantage over his adversaries in London and Paris. Also, ideological interests drove his commitment to take over Europe. British Prime Minister Neville Chamberlain underestimated Hitler's motives for conquest. Chamberlain's appeasement of Hitler only whetted the Nazi appetite for gain. Hitler may have been deterrable. Confrontation rather than appeasement might have stopped Hitler because he was in a domain of gain. Chamberlain perceived Hitler to be in a domain of loss, however, and chose appeasement over confrontation.[13]

Leaders who perceive themselves in a domain of gain are "value maximizers" who are deterrable, given the right combination of capability and resolve. It is as if gain-seekers were standing before a window of opportunity poised to jump. Leaders who perceive themselves in a domain of loss are "loss minimizers" who are not as easily deterred. It is as if they were trapped in a basement of fear and will choose high-risk options to escape. The "basement of fear" metaphor highlights the failure of classical deterrence theory to explain "irrational" decisions.

In summary, the Balkans highlight a sequence of combat and coercion that might eventuate in cooperation. The presence of combat and the prospect of cooperation raise two questions. They concern what brought the parties to the negotiating table in Dayton and what it would take to produce a lasting peace. Balancing principles might explain why the main actors came to the table and what might keep them in a state of relative peace. Finally, ancient and modern history abounds with illustrations of balancing principles that maintain the peace and security. With these general examples in mind, consider now an historical overview of Yugoslavia in particular.

CHAPTER TWO

DANCE OF THE DIPLOMATS

THE RISE OF YUGOSLAVIA

FOLLOWING THE BALKAN WARS of 1912–1913, the Ottoman Empire collapsed and Turkish rule ended in the Balkan Peninsula. Several independent political entities used the Ottoman disintegration as an opportunity to form a union. From 1914 to 1918, these units included Serbia and Montenegro; Bosnia and Herzegovina under the sovereignty of Austria-Hungary; Croatia and Slovenia, a semi-autonomous dependency of Hungary and later an Austrian crown land; and Dalmatia, a possession of Austria. In 1915, during World War I, the fighting in the Balkans began to turn against Serbia. Croat, Serb, and Slovene diplomats wrote the Declaration of Corfu, which called for a "southern Slav" state. On December 7, 1918, King Alexander of Serbia announced the creation of that state—Yugoslavia.

Six republics comprised Yugoslavia from 1946 until it fell in 1991. Then, three of the republics—Croatia, Macedonia, and Slovenia—seceded. A fourth republic, Bosnia-Herzegovina, declared its independence during 1992. And two remaining republics, Serbia and Montenegro, formed a new country dubbed "rump Yugoslavia," a small version of the federal state of Yugoslavia.[1]

THE FALL OF YUGOSLAVIA

During the 1940s, Josip Broz Tito rose as a resistance fighter against the Nazi occupation of Yugoslavia. He led an antifascist struggle with the help of a multiethnic peasantry to recreate a federal state of Yugoslavia. Tito governed Yugoslavia effectively and was able to contain the aspirations of competing ethnic groups until his death on May 4, 1980. After his death, Yugoslavia lacked a leader with Tito's personal charisma, which had held the country together. In the 1980s, the population of Yugoslavia became increasingly dissatisfied with economic conditions and labor unrest grew.

In the context of political instability, a Serbian nationalist—Slobodan Milosevic—tried to assert his authority over the entire country. But when he was elected president of Serbia in 1987, ethnic divisions began to reassert themselves. Milosevic's attempt to assert Serbian domination over the country alarmed the other republics such as Croatia.

On April 24, 1987, Milosevic gave a speech at the site of a famous battle in Serbian history in the Kosovo province of Yugoslavia. He used nationalistic rhetoric to further his own political ends. Milosevic appealed to Serbs with the slogan, "No one should be allowed to beat you." That is, Serbs should not allow ethnic Albanians in Kosovo to take advantage of them. And on September 23 and 24, 1987, Milosevic accused Ivan Stambolic, president of Serbia, of being too lenient on ethnic Albanians in Kosovo.[2] Milosevic played the ethnic card for domestic political advantage.

Two years later, Milosevic continued his verbal assault on ethnic Albanians. In a celebration of the six hundred year anniversary of the Battle of Kosovo, Milosevic spoke before thousands of Serbs. Again, the consequence of his anti-Albanian rhetoric was to strengthen his domestic political position within Serbia.[3] Milosevic's use of ethnic scapegoats in his bid for power in Serbia alarmed other nationalist leaders. One of these leaders was Franjo Tudjman of Croatia.

During the spring of 1990, Croatia's leading political party was the Democratic Union. Led by Tudjman, the party ran on the platform of self-determination within Yugoslavia. As a type of warning of what might happen if Tudjman's party were elected, Belgrade's Socialist Communist Party labeled the Democratic Union as the "Party of Dangerous Means." The implied threat was hollow, and about two-thirds of the Croatian population voted in favor of independence from Yugoslavia.

Croatia perceived Serbia's assertion of authority as a power play to dominate all of Yugoslavia and to create a Greater Serbia. Consequently, the local balance of power among the republics that was imposed by Tito dissolved. Zagreb interpreted signals sent from Belgrade as a threat to Croatia's autonomy. Zagreb reacted by imposing restrictive measures on its Serb minority in the Krajina region of Croatia. These actions included firing all Serb police officers. The Serb minority rebelled and opened fire on Croatian forces. A full outbreak of hostilities ensued. The carefully constructed balance of power among the republics and ethnic groups collapsed.

From the rational choice perspective, both Milosevic and Tudjman were actors who sought gains. Hence, the West might have deterred and coerced them. But there was little accord among Western diplomats for a policy of either deterrence or coercion. There was agreement that the behavior of Milosevic and Tudjman derived from historical ethnic hatreds. While there was some effort to deter them, the attempt lacked credibility.

U.S. DIPLOMACY: THE PARADOX OF POLICY

While Washington desired the continuation of Yugoslavia as a unitary actor, American policies contributed to its dissolution. As Yugoslavia disintegrated, the United States sent the American ambassador to Yugoslavia, Warren Zimmermann, to warn the Croats against declaring independence. On June 13, 1991, he reiterated Washington's commitment to the territorial integrity and political independence of Yugoslavia. Zimmerman presented a demarche to the effect that the United States would not tolerate the disintegration of Yugoslavia.[4] The ambassador's warning failed to prevent war for two reasons. First, the threat lacked credibility. At no time did Washington announce that any specific action would be taken if Croatia declared independence. Therefore, the American warning had no impact on Zagreb's decision to secede.

At the same time, Belgrade may have misinterpreted Zimmerman's message to Zagreb. Serbia heard what it wanted to hear: that is, the West would not intervene if Serbia chose military action to keep Yugoslavia united. In the case of Serbia, Belgrade wanted to learn that the United States would not interfere militarily with prospective efforts to hold Yugoslavia together with military force. Hence, Serbia misinterpreted the American warning to Zagreb as a go-ahead for military action. When individuals hear what they want to hear, that is an example of a motivated bias.[5]

Just as the Zimmerman visit to Croatia resulted in misinterpretations by Serbia, a visit by Secretary of State James Baker in June 1991 might have inadvertently facilitated the outbreak of war. Richard Holbrooke quotes the following from James Baker's memoirs: "My gut feeling is that we won't produce a serious dialogue on the future of Yugoslavia until all parties have a greater sense of urgency and danger. We may not be able to impart that from the outside, but we and others should continue to push."[6] Holbrooke infers that Baker was reluctant to use force because of a perception that outsiders might not succeed in compelling local actors.

Holbrooke and Baker agree that ethnic political leaders manipulate ethnicity for domestic political purposes. But the two differ on the potential for outside intervention to compel regional actors. Holbrooke was more optimistic than Baker was with respect to the role of Western threats to compel leaders in the former Yugoslavia to cease fighting and come to the table. Baker felt that a massive ground force presence would have been necessary for coercion, while Holbrooke believed that threats and air power might have been sufficient for successful coercion.

Baker warned President Tudjman that if Croatia decided to seek independence, Serbia would react with force, and the United States would refuse to aid Croatia. Belgrade saw the failure of Washington to reinforce deterrence as a green light for the Serbs to use force. In other words, the Yugoslav leadership perceived the Baker visit as a nod for the Serbs to use power to prevent a separation. Belgrade assumed that the international community did not oppose military action.

The visit by Baker was a mistake, according to the Croatian foreign minister, Mate Granic.[7] The Zimmermann and Baker demarches had a paradoxical effect: Washington desired the continuation of Yugoslavia as a unitary actor, but its policies contributed to its disintegration. The United States, however, was not alone in misreading the situation on the ground.

If diplomats interpret events in Yugoslavia as due mainly to choice or to circumstance, they leave themselves open to misunderstanding. As stated above, choice refers to the approach that explains outcomes as the result of politicians who are trying to gain advantage. Circumstance explains behavior as a result of events not under the control of politicians. A balanced approach would take into account both circumstance and choice as complementary explanations of outcomes.

Milosevic is a politician who uses ethnicity as a lever for political gain. Politicians do not create ethnic differences; but they do use them. In other words, if it were not for the circumstance of ethnic animosities, the Milosevics of the world could not choose to manipulate these differences for political advantage. Because a focus on either circumstance or choice may lead to misperception, it is wise to consider both of them.[8]

WESTERN MISPERCEPTIONS: HISTORY AND DESIRES

History and desire explain Western misperceptions in the former Yugoslavia. The perception that prior history is current destiny is an unmotivated bias: actors see now what they expect to see from historical events. On the historical front, there is the "ancient ethnic hatreds" school of thought. It dominated the foreign ministries in the Western capitals. American and European diplomats misunderstood Bosnia's past. They assumed that ancient ethnic hatreds were the underlying causes of conflict in Bosnia during the 1990s. But, in fact, ethnic groups in Yugoslavia had lived together peacefully in the past. Advocates of the ancient hatred argument, however, counter that this peaceful coexistence was only possible because of the domination of the Serbian Royal House or the Communist Party under Tito. In fact, however, despite ancient enmity, there was a period of relative peace. Because of a misreading of history, Western diplomats saw conflict in Bosnia as a result of ethnic tensions rather than external manipulation.

Desire also explains Western misperception about Yugoslavia. During the 1990s there was a tendency to overestimate the likelihood of desirable events and underestimate the occurrence of undesirable events—to engage in wishful thinking. Because of the motivated bias in perception, the allies misperceived developments in Yugoslavia. They saw what they wanted see: Yugoslavia might not disintegrate because it had been friendly to the West and antagonistic toward the Soviet Union.

In addition to history and desire, three specific factors caused Western leaders to misperceive developments in Yugoslavia: a lack of intelligence, an overemphasis on Belgrade relative to Sarajevo and Zagreb, and the view of Yugoslavia as a single economic unit. The West's lack of clear intelligence about the events in Yugoslavia was a major impediment to policymaking. There was a gap between Western perceptions of events and actual developments in the country. The Western leaders tended to emphasize the positive and de-emphasize the negative with respect to Yugoslavia. Belgrade distanced itself from Moscow; consequently, the allies assumed the best about what was happening in Yugoslavia.

Another reason for Western misperception was that the United States and its European allies dealt with Belgrade as their major interlocutor. Sarajevo and Zagreb received less attention from Western diplomats than Belgrade. Moreover, diplomats of Serbian origin filled posts in Western capitals. When the move for secession occurred in the Yugoslavian republics, Serbian diplomats downplayed this information in their representations to the West. As a result, there was a dearth of intelligence about local leaders, opposition movements, and independent journalists in the disgruntled non-Serbian republics.

Another cause of misperception concerned the economy. During the late 1980s, the West retained a vision of Yugoslavia as a unitary economic entity. There was an understanding between the Europeans and the Americans about the need to hold that economic unit together. The assumption was that market reforms and the improvement in the rights of workers would help maintain the territorial integrity and political independence of Yugoslavia.

The West continued to misinterpret events until Croatia and Slovenia expressed their strong intent to secede from Yugoslavia. The strength of their resolve and expression of their stakes could not be ignored in Western capitals. The initial allied response was to insist that Yugoslavia remain whole, despite centrifugal forces pulling it apart. U.S. policy, designed by Deputy Secretary and later Secretary of State Lawrence Eagleburger, clearly leaned toward Serbia. American policy favored the unity of Yugoslavia under Belgrade's domination, an outcome that was not acceptable to the other republics.

While tilting toward Belgrade, American and European diplomats paid less attention to Zagreb. Hence, there was less information about Croatia's attitude toward secession. Because of wishful thinking, Western policymakers tended to discount the ethnic tensions dividing the country. Eagleburger's preference for Serbia and Baker's visit to Belgrade during the summer of 1991 indicated that the United States refused to recognize the clear move toward ethnic separatism throughout the country.

The Baker-Eagleburger diplomatic approach reinforced Serbian military power. Absent the military capabilities of outside powers, the Serbian army looked formidable in contrast to the forces of the other republics. A Western arms embargo on all the republics had the least effect on Serbia as Belgrade had inherited armaments from the former Yugoslavia. In using American diplomacy to bolster Serbian military power, the United States failed to deter war. By reinforcing Belgrade's military superiority with diplomatic initiatives, Washington's actions had the effect of encouraging the use of force by the regional actors. Divided over the issue of Croatian and Slovenian secession, the parties used the American approach as a springboard for launching hostilities.

In short, unmotivated and motivated biases led to Western misperception of developments in the former Yugoslavia. The ancient ethnic hatred argument led to expectations that the current conflict might not be resolved. Belgrade's tilt away from Moscow, the view of Yugoslavia as an economic entity, and the presence of Serbian diplomatic interpreters in the West resulted in wishful thinking. An unbiased approach to the Balkans might have yielded more valid perceptions.

BONN BALANCES WASHINGTON: THE DANCE OF THE DIPLOMATS

While Washington inclined toward Belgrade, Bonn favored Zagreb. The contradictory diplomatic positions of the United States and Germany unintentionally led to the outbreak of fighting. Within Europe, an initially unified position on how to respond to Yugoslavia's crisis began to unravel shortly after the Croatian and Slovenian declarations of independence. Partly because of Bonn's tilt toward Zagreb, Germany argued that recognizing Croatia and Slovenia's independence was a way to bring an end to the fighting. Germany formally proposed recognition of Slovenia and Croatia at the European Community Council of Foreign Ministers meeting of July 4, 1991. The Community initially rejected the suggestion and Paris led the opposition to the recognition option. By the end of July, however, Bonn moved again and prospects for recognition increased due to an aborted coup in Moscow in August 1991.

Germany had originally defined its policies within the framework of the European Community and had relied on the Community's diplomatic efforts. But Bonn underestimated the risk of violent disintegration and overestimated the potential for diplomatic solution. Just as Washington engaged in wishful thinking, so did Bonn. Once the threat to Croatia had increased, however, Bonn's perception of that threat became less biased. Thereafter, Germany led European policymaking regarding Yugoslavia.

While Washington de-emphasized ethnic separatism, Germany acknowledged ethnic divisions within the country. The United States sought to resolve ethnic differences through the maintenance of Yugoslavia's territorial integrity and political unity. Germany recognized ethnic differences and wanted to partition the country along ethnic lines. At the same time, Bonn sought to balance Serbian military power with the military capabilities of Croatia and Slovenia.

While siding with Zagreb against Belgrade, Bonn cast its policies within a European framework. In doing so, Germany acted under the assumption that the international community would act as an honest broker to end hostilities. Germany believed that if the West intervened, it would do so between two independent countries—rump Yugoslavia and Croatia—rather than within the internal affairs of a single country. This argument might have been a disingenuous ploy on the part of Bonn: Germany made no effort to persuade the international community to intervene militarily in support of Croatia against Serbia. Washington's advocacy of Belgrade and Bonn's endorsement of Zagreb was a dance of the diplomats that created diplomatic deadlock. The stalemate allowed the fighting to continue in the region. The disintegration of the Soviet Union further accelerated the breakup of Yugoslavia.

The clash between Serbia and Croatia was colored with religious overtones. Orthodox Russia backed Orthodox Serbia. Germany with its large Catholic population supported Catholic Croatia. Muslim states outside the Balkans sided with the Bosnian Muslim government in Sarajevo. And the Serbs fought Croatians, Bosnian Muslim, and Albanian Muslims.[9] Religion was not the only factor in the alignments: Washington sided with the Bosnian and Kosovo Muslims over the Orthodox Serbs.

Meanwhile, on December 16, 1991, Bonn announced that it would recognize Croatia but not the former Yugoslav republic of Macedonia, thus once again dividing Yugoslavia along religious and ethnic lines. As the division proceeded, the Western reaction was one of confusion, misunderstanding, and rivalry. Historic loyalties among Western states created separate Western approaches at the expense of a concerted allied effort at conflict resolution. The West lost several opportunities to stave off the dissolution of the Yugoslav state, to impede the violence that was to follow, and to prepare the republics for independence.

TRANS-ATLANTIC DIFFERENCES:
UNITY VS. INDEPENDENCE

Why was it difficult to develop a unified policy to thwart the outbreak of war in Yugoslavia? The West never chose between two conflicting policies: continuity and unity through the support of Serbia versus change and independence through assistance to Croatia and Slovenia. The first approach emphasized the territorial integrity of the whole of Yugoslavia with Serbia as its core. The second approach acknowledged ethnic divisions within the country in the form of support for Croatian and Slovenian secession. Intra-European wrangling and transatlantic bickering produced confusion that abetted violence. The dancing of the diplomats allowed regional politicians to exacerbate ethnic tensions in order to bolster their domestic political fortunes.

Those Europeans who sided with the American approach in favor of a unified Yugoslavia felt that a violent disintegration would act as a precedent for other countries suffering from internal ethnic conflicts. Despite the German push for division of Yugoslavia, most of the rest of Europe and the United States initially offered to support the Yugoslav president, Ante Markovic, who attempted to promote market reform in the country. Countries on both sides of the Atlantic, however, overlooked the underlying political problems dividing Yugoslavia. Without a preponderance of outside military force to compel the parties to adopt a ceasefire, ethnic differences pulled them apart.

Another problem for the West was the Cold War lens through which the allies had viewed Yugoslavia. Because Tito had pulled out of the Soviet orbit, NATO members tended to perceive Yugoslavia in a favorable light, without regard to the ethnic divisions. But in the post–Cold War universe, there was no particular place for a unified Yugoslavia. Without East-West tension, the West did not value Yugoslavia's independence from the Soviet Union. Yugoslavia became a loose set of decentralized republics incapable of functioning in the new world order, its status as outside of the Soviet bloc without diplomatic significance.

Despite the changes brought about by the end of the Cold War, Western policy toward Yugoslavia sought to maintain the status quo. In doing so, the West overestimated the capacity of the Yugoslav National Army to hold back nationalist challengers. Just as the United States magnified the capabilities of the Soviet army, Washington also overestimated the capacity of the Yugoslav National Army in the post–Cold War era. The United States considered the Yugoslav National Army as a guarantor of stability against disintegration, rather than the perpetrator of instability that it became. By magnifying the capabilities of the Yugoslav National Army and assuming that it could guarantee stability, Washington added fuel to the smoldering fire that threatened to engulf the ethnic groups. Treating the Yugoslav National Army as the caretaker of Yugoslavia sent further confusing signals to the parties.

TRAFFIC SIGNALING: FAILURE TO DETER

Relying on the Serbian army as a caretaker of stability sent a faint green light to Belgrade to use force against the other republics. In order to avoid war, Washington might have sent a bright red light to the Serbs. Although the United States wanted to maintain the unity of Yugoslavia, Washington also desired to avert war. At issue, however, was the priority between these two objectives. Not only did Washington lack an agenda, NATO was also without a clear order of priorities. By wavering between a preference for unity and a desire to avoid war, the West passed up the opportunity to deter warfare.

In addition to a lack of ordered preferences, the Yugoslav conflict required sustained attention at the highest levels of authority. But Washington's attention span was short-lived. With the defeat of President Bush and election of President Clinton in 1992, the United States had turned away from global affairs to concentrate on domestic economic issues. Consequently, Washington handed Yugoslavia to the Europeans. But it soon became clear that Europe lacked the ability to marry credible threats with persuasive diplomacy. Instead, policy wrangling among the European states sent mixed signals to the Balkans, exacerbated the conflict, and failed to take advantage of occasions for diplomatic intervention.

TRAFFIC SIGNALING: IRANIAN ARMS TO THE BOSNIAN MUSLIMS

On balance-of-power grounds, it is not surprising to find ideological adversaries in tacit alignment. Such collusion is an indication that religious differences are not the only driving force behind conflicts in the Balkans. The transition from Bush to Clinton also resulted in a shift in American perception of Serbia. For the Bush administration, Belgrade was a virtual ally; but for the Clinton administration, it was a virtual foe. The change in threat perception affected Washington's view of the Bosnian Muslims. Sarajevo became the new friend, and Belgrade the new foe. Because Tehran was a friend of Sarajevo, Iran and the United States had mutuality of interests in the Balkans.

Iran and the United States had reason to align in Europe, irrespective of their differences in the Middle East. The underlying principle of such an implicit coalition is that, "The enemy of my enemy is my friend."[10] That is, Tehran and Washington confronted one another in the Persian Gulf, but stood with each other in Europe. Iran and the United States colluded to support the Bosnian Muslims against a common foe—Serbia and the Bosnian Serbs. It was as if American policymakers hoped that, "The foe (Iran) of my adversary (Serbia) is my friend."[11]

The Bosnian Muslims needed an infusion of weaponry because the international community had imposed an arms embargo on the former Yugoslavia (UN Security Council Resolution 713 of September 1991). The ostensible goal of the embargo was to stabilize the situation among the former republics. But the arms embargo left the Serbs with an unfair advantage vis-à-vis other republics, such as Bosnia. The weaponry from Tito's Yugoslav army remained with Serbia and their Bosnian Serb allies. In early April 1994, Croatian president, Franjo Tudjman, approached the Zagreb-based American ambassador, Peter Galbraith. The question was whether the United States would object to Croatia acting as a transshipment point for Iranian arms en route to Sarajevo.

The United States gave this proposition a green light when President Clinton instructed Galbraith to inform Tudjman that the ambassador had "no instructions." Washington, in effect, traded the risk of the penetration into the heart of Europe of the Iranian Revolutionary Guards for the benefit of keeping the Bosnian Muslim regime afloat. Washington's green light to Zagreb sent a signal that the United States wanted to support the Bosnian Muslims. But the resulting contentious political debate within the United States made it difficult for Washington to sustain a tacit alignment with Tehran and sent confusing messages about the intent of the United States. As a result of mixed signaling, coercive diplomacy was difficult to achieve. In addition to confused gestures, there were also neglected occasions for diplomatic progress.

MISSED OPPORTUNITIES FOR DIPLOMACY

The United States and Europe made a serious error when they did not pursue options for the peaceful resolution of the conflict in Bosnia. But where you stand on a diplomatic alternative depends on where you sit. That is, a proposal from Belgrade may have looked self-serving to the other republics, and vice versa. With this caveat in mind, consider several forgone occasions for diplomacy.

During late 1990, Bosnia, Croatia, and Slovenia indicated that they would accept a compromise solution. One idea was for Yugoslavia to evolve into a confederation with a balance among the members. Another proposed option was for a union of independent states. Primarily because of Serbia's rejection of the compromise solution, the international community disregarded this option. Serbia believed that it held a preponderance of local power and wished to maintain this status.

Belgrade advocated an alternative to a union of independent nations. It called for a restructuring of Yugoslavia's internal borders. The chief European Union negotiator, Lord Owen, believed that this proposal was the easiest way to resolve a crisis in the making.[12] Although it was initially supported by the Dutch when they held the presidency of the European Union, Owen's proposal was a nonstarter, it never got off of the ground. Owen assumed that the borders of Yugoslavia were administrative and malleable in nature but the other republics feared loss of territory to Serbia. They argued that the borders were political and inviolable. From where Sarajevo and Zagreb stood, the proposal from Belgrade looked like a ruse for a Greater Serbia.

THE HOUR OF EUROPE: SLOVENIA AND CROATIA

Following the dissolution of the Soviet Union, conflict in Bosnia presented the allies with an opportunity to fashion a European approach to crisis management. The hour of Europe had arrived. After the missed opportunities for diplomacy, fighting was a forgone conclusion. Two days after the initiation of hostilities, Europe's time in the policymaking arena continued to tick away. Under German leadership, Bonn wanted to assert a common European foreign policy for the post–Cold War era.

The way the crisis over Slovenia unfolded highlights the lack of a coherent European approach. Slovenia declared itself independent of Yugoslavia on June 25, 1991. The federal leadership and army in Belgrade wanted to subdue Ljubljana (Slovenia). But about two weeks of fighting ended with diplomatic intervention and the Brioni Accord. Under this accord, Slovenia agreed to a six-month postponement of independence, and Serbia agreed to end its war against Slovenia.

A troika of foreign ministers from the European community sealed the deal between Serbia and Slovenia. Jacques de Poos from Luxembourg, Hans van den Broek from the Netherlands, and Gianni de Michelis of Italy presided over negotiations that brought an end to the bloodshed. And on July 7, 1991, Belgrade capitulated to the trio of ministers by signing the Brioni Accord.[13] However, that agreement failed to address the more complex issue of how to maintain the peace in the absence of Great Power diplomatic intervention.

Western diplomacy correctly relied on persuasion when it was feasible, but the negotiators discounted the possibility of a resumption of violence and its expansion as a result of ethnic differences. There was diplomatic success in Slovenia because Belgrade had no real interest in maintaining Ljubljana in a Serbian-dominated Yugoslavia. Only a minuscule percentage of the Slovene population was ethnic Serb.[14]

The European Union generalized from the successful use of persuasion in the Brioni Accord to other disputes within the Balkans. It inferred from Brioni that diplomacy without force might succeed in resolving conflicts where the ethnic mix was different. In both Croatia and Bosnia, the percentage of individuals of Serbian origin is much higher than in Slovenia. Where Belgrade had a great interest in areas because the Serbian population was high, there needed to be a constant preponderance of outside force to compel compliance. Absent such a preponderance, there should have been a balance of power among the regional actors.

In contrast to Slovenia, the Serb minority in Croatia is larger,[15] comprising about 12 percent of the Croatian population. Meanwhile, the president of Croatia, Franjo Tudjman, received little if any diplomatic pressure to respect the rights of the Serb minority. Croatia's most powerful interlocutor, Germany, had already indicated that stability and not self-determination of ethnic groups was the guiding principle behind its foreign policy in that region. Following a referendum during May 1991, Croatia moved to gain its independence from federal Yugoslavia. Since becoming leader of Croatia in April 1990, however, Tudjman and the Croatian Democratic Union party had greatly alienated the Serbian minority. Irrespective of the Serbian percentage of the population in Croatia and Slovenia, European diplomacy achieved only a temporary respite with the Brioni Accord.

In conclusion, a southern Slavic state rose from the ashes of World War I and fell with the end of the Cold War. While Washington's rhetoric favored the preservation of the territorial integrity and political independence of Yugoslavia, U.S. policies facilitated its dissolution. Because of historical biases and wishful thinking, Western nations misperceived developments in Yugoslavia. Rivalry within the West was a mad dance that resulted in a diplomatic stalemate with tragic consequences for the peoples of the Balkans. Inadequate signaling by Western governments led to a failure to deter and missed opportunities for diplomatic progress. The hour of Europe to combine force with diplomacy had arrived, yet Europe had not come into agreement with regard to the Balkans.

CHAPTER THREE

AN ABORTIVE MOVE TO PREPONDERANCE

FORCEFUL DIPLOMACY REJECTED

THE FRENCH PROMOTED THE IDEA that troops from the Western European Union should be sent to Yugoslavia to guarantee peace. This was the first serious consideration of international military intervention. During September 1991, France led 35 senior officers of the Western European Union to request the creation of a Rapid Reaction Force. This combat unit would have given a tactical advantage to a peacekeeping force in the region. The officers sought armed helicopters, guns, and close air support to carry out their mission. In essence, they proposed the creation of a credible deterrent to potential military aggression in the region. Germany concurred with the French position. Bonn reasoned that the recognition of Croatia and Slovenia was of little use if the international community was not prepared to protect them.

London differed from the Bonn-Paris coalition. The British were afraid of French domination of the Western European Union. England rejected the plan of action proposed by France and Germany. The British arguments centered on the fact that there was no exit strategy and no valid reason to intervene. According to Pauline Neville-Jones, the political head of the British Foreign Office, the United Kingdom was not convinced that intervention was necessary.[1] And the UN secretary general also opposed the idea of the Rapid Reaction Force. Presumably, the United Nations did not want to change the traditional peacekeeping role of its troops. By not sending combat forces to supplement peacekeeping units, the Europeans divided force from diplomacy.

DIPLOMACY SANS FORCE: LONDON, BONN, AND PARIS

As Britain, Germany, and France were unable to agree on a military response to the crisis in Yugoslavia, they then focused on finding a political settlement. But once again, each country's concern for its own position within the European equation dominated its policy-making for a disintegrating Yugoslavia. The end result was that there was no diplomatic solution.

Differences among the Great Powers exacerbated ethnic antagonisms among the local actors. Bonn, London, and Paris each had their favorite faction within Yugoslavia. The conflict in Europe was primarily between France and Germany, but there also were disputes involving Britain. Such intra-alliance disagreements lowered the credibility of the Western resolve. The lack of resolve and the absence of force regarding Yugoslavia derived from a preoccupation among the European states to maintain a balance of power among themselves rather than to resolve conflicts in Yugoslavia. To some extent, a fear of German influence in Croatia and Slovenia drove British policy. London believed that the dissolution of Yugoslavia would give a newly united Germany an opportunity to expand its interest over those two republics. Such a contingency would make the German impact in Europe even stronger, and thereby dilute Britain's influence. London, therefore, devised a policy to balance this diplomatic threat from Bonn.

While acknowledging fears of German plans for the region, Britain's main policy aim was simply to hold Yugoslavia together. The underlying reason for London's position was its fear that if that country broke up, the dissolution would exacerbate centrifugal forces in the Soviet Union following along similar lines. In addition,

Britain was worried that once the breakup of Yugoslavia began, there would be a much larger spillover into the rest of the Balkans as well as the Caucasus. An image of falling dominoes drove London's policies toward the Slavic states—both southern and northern.

France shared the British fear of Germany. Both Britain and France chose a pro-Serb attitude in a conscious attempt to counterbalance German influences in the region. From this split, Belgrade correctly perceived that European suggestions need not be taken seriously. Hence, Europe was not in a position to engage in diplomatic persuasion. The three Great Powers of Western Europe—Bonn, London, and Paris—chose not to develop policies that would strike a balance among the players in the evolving Balkan dispute. Rather, the Great Powers jockeyed to increase their own diplomatic positions and to ensure that the balance within Europe was not disturbed by events in Yugoslavia.

In addition, other points of dissension within Europe existed. Germany claimed that its major policy aim in the Balkans was stability, which it favored over ethnic self-determination. The desire for independence of the Krajina Serbs of Croatia and, subsequently, the Serbs of Bosnia had to be subjugated to a more vital aim— European stability. Although Germany favored secession for the republics of Slovenia and Croatia, Bonn did not favor independence for national minorities within them. Because the big three of Europe divided over ethnic-based claims, they also differed over political independence for the republics.

In contrast to Germany, France believed that ethnic self-determination was the most important consideration. According to Christian Reuilly, the head of the Bosnian policy desk at the French Foreign Ministry, France was deeply sympathetic to Serb minorities who refused to live in countries dominated by other ethnic groups.[2] He believed the West had no right to dictate that the Serb people must live in five different countries. France's policy toward Yugoslavia assumed that Serb minorities had certain rights, including perhaps the right to secede from a republic within a disintegrating nation-state. Moreover, French President Francois Mitterand's personal regard for Serbia had a strong impact on that country's policy toward Yugoslavia. As a French *resistant,* Mitterand had fought against the

Nazis. Consequently, he empathized with the Serbs. They were, in his eyes, still the *partisans* who had fought so valiantly against fascism in World War II.

Europe's failure to solve the Yugoslav crisis also stems from an inherent weakness within the European diplomatic structure. The European Union aspires to a common foreign policy, but this diplomatic unity proved to be a myth as events surrounding the eventual recognition of Slovenia and Croatia demonstrate. Perhaps because the union lacked its own policy derived from a consensus among the members, it adopted the German approach. When Bonn decided it would push for immediate recognition of the independence of Croatia and Slovenia, the European Union adhered to that policy.

Consider the political events in Germany and Europe during 1990–1991 in order to understand Bonn's role in the Yugoslav crisis. According to Hans Ulrich-Seidt of the Yugoslav desk in the Foreign Office in Bonn, German foreign policy was driven by the instability in the Soviet Union.[3] During the summer of 1991, there were still four hundred thousand Soviet troops in East Germany. Therefore, Germany decided that the aim of its approach to the Soviet Union would be stability. If stability could not be achieved on the national level, Germany decided to aim for the next level. Because the Soviet Union as an entity was disintegrating, Germany would aim for a stable Russia, Ukraine, and Belarus. The Germans also applied this policy to Czechoslovakia as well as Yugoslavia.

As Yugoslavia disintegrated, moreover, there was domestic pressure on the German Foreign Office to be more active than it was during the Gulf War. According to critics of the government, Germany had played too passive a role in the Gulf War. In response, the government rejected "checkbook diplomacy" for Yugoslavia and both the left and the right pushed for diplomatic action.

A right-wing party in Germany, the Christian Democratic Union (CDU), put pressure on Bonn to stop the fighting between the Serbs and the Slovenes. The CDU expressed alarm particularly because its large constituency in Bavaria (southern Germany) was just under four hours away via Austria from the fighting in Slovenia. Therefore, Germany felt especially vulnerable. The German media took up the cause as well and put pressure on the government to offer substantial political support to Slovenia and Croatia.

Foreign Affairs Minister Hans-Dietrich Genscher faced a veritable coalition demanding a strong German hand to resolve the Yugoslav crisis. A right-of-center daily newspaper regularly featured the writings of Johann Georg Reismuller, who opposed Belgrade's protection of ethnic Serbs in other provinces.[4] He held that Nazi Germany had adopted the notion of the "ubermensch," a greater state. This idea assumed that Berlin had an obligation to protect Germans wherever they lived. Just as Berlin claimed a "Greater Germany," Belgrade asserted a Greater Serbia. Belgrade would assume responsibility for protecting Serbs wherever they lived. Thus, Serbs in the Krajina region of Croatia would fall under the safekeeping of Belgrade. Reismuller strongly opposed the "ubermensch," of Belgrade. Furthermore, he was particularly fervent in his support for Croatia. With his extraordinary influence on decisionmakers in Bonn, Reismuller added his weight to the move toward recognizing Croatia.

Foreign Minister Genscher became increasingly susceptible to public opinion pressures. Even the revered leader, the former chancellor, Willy Brandt, rejected "Yugoslavism," or the Serbian attempt to extend its authority over the whole of the former Yugoslavia. Brandt criticized Bonn for overestimating the principle of noninvolvement. In light of the public pressure, the German Foreign Office knew it had to take some action.

However, because Germany had maintained the same position as its European neighbors and the United States until 1991, it was difficult to make a unilateral change in policy. Nevertheless, Bonn began an about-face in favor of the secessionist states. The Foreign Office insisted that its actions in Yugoslavia must be seen in relation to what was happening in the former Soviet Union, rather than simply in the context of internal political pressures in Yugoslavia. If dissolution were inevitable, Bonn argued, then it should be done in a stable manner. Hence, Germany wanted the European Union to recognize Croatia and Slovenia as independent states. Germany had one major strategic aim when it pushed for recognition of these two republics: self-sustained stability for the new republics in the Balkans and in the Soviet Union.

Another policy goal of Germany was to include the United States in the conflict resolution process. According to Hans Dietrich Seidt of the German Foreign Office, the French and British were unprepared to acknowledge the reality of what was happening on the ground and the German Foreign Office recognized the need for American intervention to prod Europe to take actions it would not take alone.[5] Bonn felt that the 1990 reunification of Germany and the Potsdam agreement of 1945 that had dictated the rules of engagement for four-and-a-half decades in Europe had broken down.

The rules of the game that evolved in accordance with the Yalta and Potsdam agreements following the Second World War divided Europe into spheres of influence among Great Britain, the Soviet Union, and the United States. Under the Potsdam Agreement, the former German territories lying east of the Rivers Oder and Neisse came under Polish sovereignty. The accord shifted Poland's frontier with the Soviet Union westward. Poland become a "people's democracy" on the Soviet model, and Lithuania began to be treated again as a part of the Soviet Union. Also, United States occupation forces oversaw the disarmament and demilitarization of Japan.

But with the impending dissolution of the Soviet Union, Paris and London were concerned that the Yalta and Potsdam balance of power within Europe was disrupted. France and Great Britain recognized that they were unable to act without a push from across the Atlantic. The French and British suspected that the German recognition of Slovenia and Croatia was a result of an intense drive toward German domination of "Mittleuropa," the former Eastern bloc. By recognizing Croatia, Paris and London would reinforce German policy. Diplomatic recognition of Croatia would also imply protection of that former republic by the international community. Such recognition was not a surrogate for military intervention, however, without an explicit commitment from the powers to defend Croatia.

Even with the hesitation of London and Paris, Bonn pursued its course and decided to threaten unilateral recognition if the European Union (EU) refused to join in the German initiative. Just before the

European Community (EC) Summit set for December 16, 1991, UN Secretary General Javier Perez de Cuellar sent a letter appealing to Genscher to halt plans for the premature, selective, and discordant recognition, which Perez believed would bring about fighting in the rest of Yugoslavia. The United States also tried to block Germany.

Finally, the EC established a committee chaired by Robert Badinter. Its mission was to decide whether the Yugoslav republics complied with the minority protection criteria that the EC requires to grant recognition to independent states. Croatia fell short of the criteria but even so, at Germany's urging, the European Community recognized Croatia and Slovenia before Christmas of 1991.

Did recognition come too soon? Premature recognition is a commonly accepted criticism of the Western response to Yugoslavia's breakup. In fact, however, perhaps recognition came too late. Had Croatia been recognized right after the referendum and after its proclamation of independence in June 1991, the conflict might not have been seen as an internal civil war. The Serbian attacks would have been seen as outright foreign aggression against a state. So recognition of Croatia as an independent state might have been another way to prevent military conflict. Germany's insistence on the recognition of Slovenia and Croatia renewed Germany's stature as a power broker on the international scene. Bonn's success, however, also solidified the fears of other European countries concerning German designs for southeastern and middle Europe. Contrary to these fears, Germany, having achieved what it set out to do, effectively withdrew from the international group involved with Bosnia. Bonn left London, Paris, and Washington with the task of trying to put out the sparks that eventually ignited in Bosnia.

WESTERN MILITARY INTERVENTION: PEACEKEEPING FORCES

After the ill-timed recognition, the only credible threat the West could use to end violence in the former Yugoslavia was force. When military action came, however, it was not in the form of an interventionist force, which might have provided a credible threat to the belligerents, but rather a peacekeeping force with scant capabilities. In February 1992, the United Nations passed Security Council Resolution 743, which set up a Protection Force (UNPROFOR) and created three United Nations Protected Areas (UNPAs).

It was assumed that the UNPAs placed in Croatia would provide a credible threat to any party that chose to engage in military action. However, UNPROFOR was seriously hampered by restrictions placed on the number and types of military equipment it was allowed to use. The guidelines permitted no more than 15 armored personnel carriers. The most serious drawback of UNPROFOR's mandate was that impartiality required neutrality. Subsequently, UNPROFOR troops were able to do little to affect the course of the fighting in Croatia, and later Bosnia.

UNPROFOR's deployment was preceded by one of the most controversial Western decisions taken during the Yugoslav crisis—the September, 1991 passage of United Nations Security Council Resolution 713, which placed an arms embargo on the whole of the former Yugoslavia. The quarantine was designed to limit the influx of arms to all parties in the region. Instead, it tipped the military advantage dangerously toward the Serbs, which increased rather than decreased the likelihood of war in Bosnia.

Without a strong military presence from the outset, the European negotiating position weakened. The leverage Europeans used was meant to be a combination of the promise of rewards and the threat of punishments. Unfortunately, the belligerents understood very early on that the threats were not credible. In 1991, the European troops operated under a zero-kill policy that translated into taking no causalities, and taking few risks.

The lack of a credible military response paved the way for the fighting in Bosnia. Had the West intervened militarily during the shelling of Dubrovnik or Vukovar, there is every indication that the Serb factions in Bosnia, as well as the Serb leadership in Belgrade, might have sought a negotiated settlement in Bosnia. Many observers from Britain to Croatia to France interviewed for this book believe that limited airstrikes during the shelling of Vukovar and Dubrovnik would have been sufficient to stop the spread of the war.

Why was military action not taken? According to British diplomat Alain Charleton, it would have been impossible for the Europeans to intervene without the leadership of the United States. Croatia certainly wanted stronger American engagement, but this was not forthcoming.

Although, according to Gojko Susak, Croatia's defense minister, even if Europe had not been willing to help Croatia, the United States indicated that it would have been willing to help but was hindered by the arms embargo.[6] The Americans, said Susak, were afraid that the press would find out if they broke the embargo. In addition, the Americans were politically, diplomatically, and conceptually detached from the events in Europe. Some analysts even argue that the United States was following a conscious attempt to put the Europeans in the embarrassing situation of being unable to resolve the crisis. Another thesis maintains that the European Union was using the Yugoslav crisis as a tool to assert the European Union as an essential international entity that would eventually bring Russia into its fold and keep the Americans out.

FROM SLOVENIA AND CROATIA TO BOSNIA

From an initial focus on Slovenia and Croatia, the hostilities in the Balkans shifted to Bosnia. Underlying both theaters of engagement were two questions that divided Europe and created a fault line between Europe and America: Were hostilities in Bosnia a civil war among ethnic groups claiming legitimate rights to self-determination?[7] Or were the hostilities a war of Serbian aggression against independent states like Slovenia, Croatia, and Bosnia? Western countries provided different answers to these questions.

Those who supported the territorial integrity of the whole of Yugoslavia or preferred a loose confederation under Serbian domination initially called the hostilities a civil war. Those who favored political independence for the republics and opposed the concept of a Greater Serbia described the fighting as an international war. Britain opposed Serbia during the late 1990s. In the early part of that decade, however, London supported Belgrade and used the term "civil war" to describe conflict in the Balkans. Germany leaned toward Slovenia and Croatia and led the camp employing the term "international war."

According to Mirza Hajric, the government of Bosnia's adviser for international relations and foreign affairs, it was Britain's insistence that the conflict was a civil war that was most damaging to the Bosnian government's position.[8] Hajric believes that Britain followed a misguided policy based on the idea that the war would last only three to six months, or that war exhaustion would lead the parties to come to the table.[9] Hajric asserts that Britain refused to accept Bosnian claims that Serbia transferred whole weapons from Yugoslavia to Serb factions within Bosnia. At the same time, Britain's policy was to ensure that no one party was labeled "victim." In so doing, no moral pressure would be placed on Europe to defend that victim.

The best Europe could offer was to extend the United Nations Protection Force (UNPROFOR) from Croatia into Bosnia, a step that was taken on September 14, 1992. UNPROFOR's mission was to protect humanitarian convoys provided by the United Nations high commissioner for refugees. Once again, this military intervention was not designed to deter fighting or coerce a settlement. Too little and too late, the proposal may have even have facilitated a continuation of the conflict in Bosnia.

Because lack of resolve ruled out Western intervention with combat forces in Bosnia—the only solution that might have coerced the parties to end their fighting—Europe and the United Nations turned its attention to a negotiated settlement via diplomatic persuasion. Between May and December 1992, the parties convened the London conference, the most ambitious international meeting on Bosnia to date including 30 countries and organizations. The assembly called for restoration of territory taken by force and condemnation of Serb aggression. It also reaffirmed the international community's commitment to a multiethnic Bosnia. Additionally, the conference tightened sanctions against Belgrade and stationed monitors along Serbia's international frontiers. However, this approach proved to have little weight without the supporting threat of military action.

With respect to sanctions, Bonn consistently favored better-enforced punishment against Serbia and sought to isolate Serbia diplomatically by suspending its membership to international institutions. Regarding the lifting of the Western arms embargo on the republics of the former Yugoslavia, Bonn had hinted that it favored this option as early as January 1993, but was torn between its most important partners—London and Paris—and found it hard to establish a clear position.

VANCE-OWEN PEACE PLAN

While European diplomats danced around the problem, the Bush administration threatened to use force. On December 25, 1992, President Bush sent a letter to President Slobodan Milosevic[10] serving notice that he was willing to use U.S. troops to protect members of UN peacekeeping forces in Bosnia. If the Security Council voted to step up enforcement of the no-fly zone (NFZ) it imposed over Bosnia during 1992, Washington was willing to back up the council with ground forces. But the American move to use force in the Balkans lost momentum when the designated peacemakers suggested that force and diplomacy did not go hand in hand. Two key diplomatic envoys called on the UN Security Council to drop its push to toughen enforcement and give diplomatic efforts more of a chance. The two diplomats were Lord David Owen, former British foreign secretary, who represented the European Community presidency and former U.S. secretary of state, Cyrus Vance, who represented the United Nations.

On January 12, 1993, the two envoys presented the Vance-Owen peace plan, which created ten autonomous provinces based largely on ethnic mix. For the next five months, negotiations among Muslims, Croats, and Serbs were undertaken to gain acceptance of this plan, known as the VOPP.[11] Croatian diplomats described this plan as the best solution for a peaceful settlement, but it ultimately failed.[12] Although Vance and Owen explicitly requested that force not be used to back up their diplomacy, the threat of force might have been useful to their efforts.

Recall one of the themes of this analysis: in the context of a credible preponderance of external power, diplomacy has an opportunity to bring local warring actors to the table. And, if there is a balance of power among them, diplomatic persuasion by external parties has a chance of gaining the compliance of the antagonists to a lasting peace. But the manner in which the Vance-Owen negotiations proceeded gave a clear indication of a preference for a local balance of power among the belligerents rather than a preponderance of outside power, which would have allowed coercive diplomacy to succeed.

Consider the treatment of three local officials at the international bargaining table. Alija Izetbegovic was the duly elected president of Bosnia-Herzegovina, an internationally recognized state present at a negotiating session organized under the auspices of the Vance-Owen peace process; Radovan Karadzic was the leader of Republica Srpska, the self-declared Bosnian Serb entity; and Milan Babic represented the Croats. In an effort to strike a balance among all three representatives, the forum stripped Izetbegovic of the treatment he normally would have received as head of state.

Vance and Owen placed Izetbegovic at the same level as the other representatives, despite numerous protests from the government of Bosnia. By insisting on this arrangement, Vance and Owen, in essence, denied that government its legitimacy to represent the entire nation. They reduced Izetbegovic to the role of representative of the ethnic Muslim population of the country, although the Bosnian government had been elected as head of a multiethnic government. This balancing act had the effect of creating equals in a situation that did not merit it.

Even so, the Bosnian Muslims and the Bosnian Croats accepted the Vance-Owen Peace Plan. At a meeting in Athens, Radovan Karadzic also eventually signed the package but with the proviso that the agreement had to be ratified by the Bosnian Serb parliament, which called for a referendum. That referendum, held on May 15–16, 1993, rejected the VOPP by a vote of 96 percent of the Bosnian Serb population.

One of the major unanswered questions regarding the Bosnian conflict is who was responsible for the failure of the plan. According to Lord Owen, the blame can be placed squarely at the feet of the Americans.[13] Lord Owen argues that the plan was sabotaged by the Clinton administration and that Washington's policy concerning the VOPP was confused from the beginning. After initial support, the United States began speaking of an alternative strategy, "lift and strike"—lift the arms embargo and launch airstrikes on Serb targets. In other words, Washington began speaking in terms of a military threat at the same time that Europe was attempting to use persuasion. The European position was considerably weakened as a result.

After much wavering, the Americans finally decided on a policy that recognized the Muslims as victims and the Serbs as aggressors. At a crucial junction when support for the VOPP should have been forthcoming, the Americans, instead, began to present arguments stating that the plan rewarded the Serbs for their aggression. This, Owen claims, is due to sophisticated public relations campaigning by the Bosnian government.

At the same time, according to Owen, the Bosnian government began to believe that the Americans would intervene on their behalf and decided it would be in their benefit to continue the war rather than end it with the implementation of VOPP. Mirza Hajric, of the Bosnian government, however, contends that the Owen view is false:

> We [in Bosnia] never had any promise that the Americans would step in militarily. During the campaign, Clinton called for airstrikes. But as soon as he did become President, it was clear that he would not militarily intervene. But what is correct is that Owen believes that we used public relations much better than the others did, and that we used that method to attract attention to our problem and portray ourselves as the victims.[14]

According to supporters of the VOPP, the United States was drawing support away from the plan and was trying to convince the Bosnian government that it was not in their best interest to go along with the VOPP. But the government of Bosnia states that Washington did not launch a concerted effort to push Sarajevo to withdraw support. The Bosnian position is that they did not think the plan was perfect but were willing to accept it because any further delays would result in more casualties. The major problem in the VOPP, according to both the Americans and the Bosnians, is that it did not preserve the multiethnic quality of the country. Nonetheless, more

than three years later, when the Dayton Accords were finally implemented, Bosnia lost its multiethnic composition forever.

Croatian Foreign Minister Mate Granic argues that Owen's
most serious problem is that he did not understand the mindset and
ambitions of the Serbian leader Slobodan Milosevic.[15] Therefore not
enough pressure was put on Milosevic, despite UN applied sanctions, to bring an end to the fighting. According to Granic, lack of
coercive pressure was a major explanation why the VOPP failed and
the Dayton Accords succeeded. The Vance-Owen team negotiated
directly with Karadzic, not realizing perhaps that the real power
broker Milosevic, was in Belgrade. When Karadzic could not or
would not deliver Serb participation in the VOPP, the plan simply
failed. The West had no leverage and no bargaining tools to force a
Serb acceptance of the plan.

In retrospect, Owen argues that the peace plan should have
been implemented without the consent of all parties involved. Implementation, however, would have necessitated a military force of
some stature being sent to Bosnia as peacemakers, not as peacekeepers. Sending troops to make peace was a move no Western
country was willing to undertake unilaterally or as part of a multi-
state force.[16]

London blames both the Bosnian Serbs as well as the Americans
for the failure of the Vance-Owen Plan. Alain Charleton argues that
Karadzic reneged on the plan because he felt that the Americans
would not provide the type of military support necessary to implement the plan.[17] Charleton also argues that it would have been ex-
tremely difficult to implement the VOPP, that the document was
flawed from the start. Without U.S. military and political support
firmly behind the VOPP, any chance of successful implementation
was doomed.

The most compelling explanation for why the Vance-Owen
peace plan failed has less to do with the absence of American support and more to do with the lack of incentives for Serbs to negotiate. There was no credible threat of retaliation menacing the Serbs
if they rejected the VOPP. The carrot was peace in Bosnia. But without the creation of an independent Serb state, it was an insufficient
incentive for the Bosnia Serbs and their mentors in Belgrade. Again,

the refusal to place pressure on the Serbs to accept the VOPP with credible threats is, according to the Bosnians, indicative of the over-all European tendency to be pro-Serb throughout the conflict.[18]

SAFE HAVENS

The international community, temporarily powerless as one or more parties in the conflict rejected subsequent plans, decided to focus its attention on the protection of civilians. On June 4, 1993, the United Nations Security Council adopted Resolution 836, which mandated that UNPROFOR defend UN declared safe havens. This action would clearly demonstrate the full impotency of Western intervention in Bosnia.

The establishment of safe havens under the auspices of the United Nations proved that the United Nations was unable to protect civilians. On May 23, 1993, the foreign ministers of Britain, France, Spain (which had troops in Bosnia), the United States, and Russia issued the Joint Action Programme. It called for the creation of six safe areas around the Muslim enclaves of Sarajevo, Gorazde, Zepa, Srebencia, Tuzla, and Bihac. Rather than insisting on or even imposing a political solution on all three sides in the conflict, the West would instead try to protect the civilians.

Alain Charleton of the British Foreign Office underlined British opposition to the safe haven resolution.[19] He said that the idea for safe havens stemmed from the successful international intervention with the Kurds in northern Iraq. Because of the relatively clear line of separation between the Iraqi army and the Kurdish population, Western countries could monitor Baghdad's armed movement toward the Kurds entirely from the air. However, the varied locations of safe havens in Bosnia required a groundforce peacekeeping presence. In fact, there was no way to guarantee that these places could be defended without troops on the ground.

In order to protect the six safe areas, the United Nations insisted that it needed over 36,000 troops. Instead, the deployment only included a few thousand troops. The UN safe havens were, in fact, simply a bluff. The UN could only hope that Serbs would not take the safe areas which, of course, they eventually did.

Why did the United Nations not protect the safe areas? Most of the European countries participating in the Bosnia peacekeeping operation had a zero-kill policy. That is, no casualties under any circumstances. Hence, forces protecting the safe areas were not a credible threat. When the Serbs began to move in on several of the safe havens, the "protection forces" simply withdrew, in one case, under the cover of the night. According to General Phillipe Morillon, who went further than any other UN commander in attempting to defend the safe havens, the problem was that the West simply refused to use force.[20] The zero-kill policy has become a fragile point for democracies. It leaves troops lacking the proper means to carry out missions.

Another problem, according to General Morillon, is that the troops operating under the command of the United Nations were actually under the ultimate authority of their own respective sovereign states. When fighting intensified around the Gorazde safe haven, for example, London ordered British troops to withdraw. The lesson was a painful one for the British, according to Alain Charleton: "Never promise what you cannot keep."[21] One might amend that to: "Never promise what was never intended to be kept in the first place."

In addition to Gorazde, there was a massacre in Srebenica. It is undoubtedly one of the most severe indictments of Western involvement in the Bosnian conflict. Bosnian Serbs killed thousands of Muslims after the UN troops—some eight hundred Dutch soldiers—withdrew. The West was largely discredited because of its refusal to defend the safe havens.

Pauline Neville-Jones claims that the British found themselves in an impossible situation regarding Srebenica.[22] She said that the safe havens effectively kept the Serbs out until the commander of the Serbs, Mladic, "went mad." He began to see that the Bosnian Serbs were about to lose the war, and, when the balance of power tipped against him, he changed his strategy. Attacking the safe havens was a strategic move on the Bosnian Serb part. They wanted to do away with Muslim enclaves, and knew that the international community did not have the will to stop them.

On February 4, 1994, Bosnian Serb forces shelled the Sarajevo marketplace, resulting in numerous civilian deaths. Four days later, the United Nations requested NATO airstrikes. These compelled the Bosnian Serbs to withdraw their heavy weapons from the Sarajevo zone.

CONTACT GROUP PLAN

On the negotiating front, the foreign ministers of France, Russia, Britain, the United States, and Germany formed the Contact Group, which Italy later joined. Its peace plan proposed dividing Bosnia into two sections—51 percent for the Bosnian Federation (composed of the Bosniacs—Bosnian Muslims—and Croats) and 49 percent for the Bosnian Serbs. The Bosnian Serb Republica Srpska Assembly rejected this plan on August 3, 1994. Despite the failure of the Contact Group plan, one important element had changed in the negotiating pattern—the Americans were now active participants, and increasingly making their voices heard.

According to Susak, the Croatian defense minister, the American and European policymaking approaches were strikingly different.[23] He held that the European policy reflects an inability to choose. But the American policy reflects a sort of pragmatic decisionmaking. When the Americans sense something, they make a decision and then follow it. Susak believed the Europeans ultimately played a small part in the Bosnian conflict. It was the Americans who mattered.

In the eyes of Croatian officials, Europe had lost its credibility and what had once been the hour of Europe had by now become America's hour. Washington became actively involved in the Bosnian crisis when the inter-European power play endangered the overall relations between the United States and Europe and when it became pointedly obvious that the European approach to ending the war in Bosnia was futile.

Hido Biscevic, the senior policy analyst at the Croatian Foreign Ministry, believes the United States became involved in the Balkans once it became obvious that Russia still posed a security threat to countries of concern to the West.[24] He said that the United States realized that the dissolution of the former Soviet Union did not open a new historical phase in international relations. By 1994, there was a rising understanding in the United States that the Cold War might be over but the Cold Peace had taken its place. Russian policy had not changed substantially. Moscow may have withdrawn for ideological and economic reasons from the Baltics and Central Europe, but Russia was trying to reassert itself in the Balkans and the Caucasus. Washington understood that the former Yugoslavia was a most sensitive area in terms of building a new European security structure.

At this time, there was a security gap spreading from the Baltics to the Adriatic. At issue was not only a question of relations among London and Bonn, Paris and Washington, Bonn and Zagreb, as well between Sarajevo and Washington. Rather, the composition of the security architecture for the post–Cold War era was at stake. Not only had the fighting in Bosnia destabilized the regional balance within Europe, but the international balancing equation was also in danger of being upset.

Washington recognized the need to provide security and stability in the zone that runs along the border of the former Soviet Union including the Baltics, Central Europe, former Yugoslavia, and the Caucuses. Meanwhile, the Europeans did not seem to recognize the broader international implications of the security vacuum in the region. The Croats believed that the European approach, particularly the French and British, accommodated Russia by implementing a pro-Serbian policy. This policy affected the entire region because by appeasing Russia and Serbia, the Europeans needed to accommodate the other Orthodox state in the region—Greece, which was a key partner for the Serbs.

The future relationship between Russia and the European Union, or Russia and the United States will greatly determine the course of history in the twenty first century. If the United States develops a special relationship with Russia, Europe's growth might be hindered. If the EU develops that special relationship, then Brussels would increase in international stature and the EU would have the

potential to become a prevailing economic and political force in the
world. So neither side was willing to call Russia's bluff and take a
stronger stance against the Serbs until Russia became a partner in
the negotiations.

The division among the outside powers played into the hands of
the local actors. While the British supported Serbia to some degree,
there is also little doubt that the American strategy was to empower
the Croats. The Croatian Foreign Ministry believes that Europe
wanted to see Serbia as an inevitable regional power. One analysis
is that Europe advocated the balancer idea of regional stability and
chose Serbia to hold the balance between the other regions. The
Americans had an alternative vision whereby the Bosnian Muslims
and the Croats together balanced Serbian power. This concept of a
balance of power among the republics is the basic idea behind the
Dayton Accords.

The balance of power angled away from the Serbs and toward
the federation of Bosnia and Croatia on August 4, 1995, when
Croatia launched Operation Storm to oust the Serbian population
in the Krajina region of the country. The majority of Serbs fled via
Bosnia into Serbia. Consider the views of Mate Granic, the Croatian foreign minister.[25] He said that the United States never gave implicit approval to the Croats to undertake Operation Storm (the
Krajina operation), but it was clear to him that if the Croats could
take the Krajina in seven days or fewer, there would be no serious
pressure from the West, specifically from Washington. The Germans
had by this time reentered the political scene surrounding Bosnia.
But Bonn was also reluctant to issue any real threat to the Croatians
regarding their military action in the Krajina.

The most important shift at this point was that for the first
time, the Americans offered a credible threat to the Serbs. NATO
agreed to launch airstrikes and the Croats proved capable of
launching a lightning speed military operation against the Serbs in
Krajina, who received no support from Belgrade. Milosevic failed
to provide support because of fears that economic sanctions would
be tightened. Now it was Washington that was determining the
strategy on how to end the war rather than the Europeans, who

were more concerned about how to find a consensus among their respective national positions.

What made the American approach so effective was the offer of a credible balance to the Serb military machine. This balance was created by providing the Bosnian Muslims—who were inferior militarily to the other two parties—with a strong military partner, Croatia. The alignment formed the basis for the Bosnia-Croatian federation. Even though it was effective, the Europeans were not happy with the American approach.

Alain Charleton explains why there was dissatisfaction with the United States.[26] He held that there was a strain in the relationship between London and Washington caused by the differences in the two countries' approaches. The then British foreign secretary, Douglas Hurd, believed that the United States needed to get into the diplomatic game and have American troops on the ground. However, once Washington became involved diplomatically, it was still not prepared to deploy American forces.

For the Europeans, it became an impossible situation. Washington was calling the shots politically but was unwilling to place troops on the ground. Consequently, retaliation following any concerted Western military action against the Bosnian Serbs would be directed at European troops—primarily French and British—who were on the ground. The French also clashed with the Americans over the gap between an increasingly assertive U.S. diplomacy and the absence of American forces.

Despite the lack of American ground forces, however, U.S. diplomacy began to have an effect. That the war in Bosnia changed course once the Americans arrived on the diplomatic scene is largely a reflection of the inadequacy of the security structure for Europe in the post–Cold War era. Europe's military power had been dedicated to opposing the Soviet Union, and the Americans controlled most of the nuclear potential. Because it was unlikely that conflict in the Balkans would escalate into nuclear war, American diplomatic involvement was not as great as it would have been during the Cold War. Even without the fear of nuclear conflict, however, Washington decided to involve itself in stabilizing the Balkans.

PREPONDERANCE OF POWER
AND COERCIVE DIPLOMACY

It was not until Washington spearheaded NATO military operations with diplomatic activity that the parties signed the Dayton Peace Agreement of December 1995. Prior to the systematic use of military force, the Serbs could not be kept in check. NATO airpower and Croatian military success on the ground were two factors that made for a preponderance of credible power.[27]

The application of Western military force took the form of a NATO operation, Deny Flight, which took place from April 12, 1993, to December 20, 1995.[28] For nearly one thousand days, Deny Flight prevented the warring parties from using airpower. The mission had three parts: to setup a no-fly zone (NFZ), to protect "safe areas," and to support UN peacekeeping troops on the ground.[29]

To create the NFZ, NATO forces monitored and enforced compliance with UN Security Council Resolution (UNSCR) 816, which banned flights by fixed-wing and rotary-wing aircraft in the airspace of Bosnia.[30] To protect the safe areas, the UN Security Council Resolution 836 provided NATO with the authority to conduct airstrikes against designated targets threatening the security of the UN-declared safe areas. The third aspect of the NATO mission was to protect UN troops on the ground. Resolution 981 authorized the provision of close air support for UN peacekeeping forces. On December 20, 1995, the NATO-led multinational Implementation Force (IFOR) assumed responsibility for the military aspects of the Dayton Peace Agreement on Bosnia.

With respect to Croatian military success on the ground, the newly trained and equipped Croatian army of 100,000 troops launched an all out offensive against 50,000 "rebel" Serbs in Krajina in August 1995.[31] In a four-day blitz, Croatia's army regained 20 percent of Croatian territory that had been seized by the Serbs. The offensive struck along a 700-mile line, piercing Krajina in 30 places. In that same month, Croat forces also helped the Muslims take two towns in Bosnia formerly controlled by the Bosnian Serbs.

As a result of the convergence of NATO airpower and Croatian military successes on the ground, Dayton succeeded in bringing the parties to the table.[32] Although it did not permanently stop the fighting, Dayton resulted in a temporary continuation of a ceasefire among the parties and prevented them from resuming hostilities. Prior peace plans were not as successful as Dayton because NATO had not used force as a prelude to diplomacy.

In the context of the use of Western military force, consider again the peace plans. The pre-Dayton proposals, Vance-Owen, Owen-Stoltenberg, and the Contact Group Plan, did not benefit from NATO military action. The Vance-Owen Peace Plan of October 1992 called for the division of Bosnia into ten ethnically based provinces.[33] These provinces together would have composed one state within the internationally recognized preconflict borders of Bosnia. Three provinces would have gone to each ethnic group—the Serbs, the Croats, and the Muslims respectively. And the tenth would be the free city of Sarajevo. These provinces would have had autonomy over cultural policy and a weak federal government.

The Owen-Stoltenberg plan of June 1993 proposed the creation of a tripartite confederation of Bosnia split along ethnic lines. The Serbs would have received 52.5 percent of the territory comprised of two large areas connected by a wide Posavina Corridor. The Croats would have received 17.5 percent comprised of two areas both adjacent to Croatia—one in the north by the city of Brcko, and the other in western Herzegovina including the town of Mostar. The Muslims would have received 30 percent comprised of four different enclaves. The Contact Group Plan of July 1994 based the division of territory on a 49/51 percent split to the Bosnian Serbs and to the Muslim-Croat federation respectively.[34]

The Dayton Peace Agreement of December 1995 created a unified Bosnia-Herzegovene state composed of two entities, a Muslim Croat federation and the Srpska Republic of Bosnia-Herzegovina.[35] The central government of the unified state would have its own presidency and a parliament that would be representative of the ethnic make-up of the country. Two-thirds of the seats would go to the Muslim Croat federation and one-third would go to the Srpska Republic. Additionally, the Bosnian Serb Republic would elect a national assembly and a President, and the federation would establish a House of Representatives.

The Dayton Peace Agreement addressed the goal of the Bosnian Muslims for a unified state and a functional central government within internationally recognized borders. The agreement addressed the Bosnian Serb goal of having an independent entity with the right to self-determination. Dayton also gave the Serbs a viable corridor, and thus a unified territory.

Two approaches explain why prior diplomatic efforts fell short and Dayton hit the mark. One assumes that in situations where power is balanced among the parties, diplomatic persuasion is the only realistic bargaining tool. Diplomacy without force was the approach followed by negotiators until Dayton. The second school presupposes that an imbalance of power allows for a strategy of credible threats of punishment and/or promises of reward to complement persuasion. With America serving as the principal "imbalancer," NATO was finally able to coerce the parties and bring armed hostilities to an end.

Although the international community imposed a cessation of violence, this state of affairs is a "no war, no peace" situation. At issue is how to prevent a war scenario from recurring and to move toward genuine peace. The presence of NATO ground forces can maintain the ceasefire while the parties learn the benefits of voluntary cooperation among themselves. Hence, a next step is for the international community to reaffirm its military presence on the ground while taking into account the role ethnicity plays in the conflict.

INTERNATIONAL WAR AND ETHNIC CONFLICTS

Dayton reflects the desire of the ethnic groups to live as separate entities. Consider the attitude toward separateness by one member of a focus group from the city of Mostar, a part of the federation of Bosnia and Croatia. He stated, "The time has come for the brothers to split up. Slovenia seceded, Croatia has its own, Serbia has its own, and now these brothers in Bosnia Herzegovina need to split up so that it is clear what belongs to whom." A USIA poll conducted in January 1997 found 91 percent of the Bosnian Serbs and 84 percent of the Bosnian Croats in agreement with the statement, "It would be better for us to be independent than to remain part of Bosnia."[36]

Dayton addressed the issue of separateness head-on by developing two entities: the Serb dominated Republika Srpska and the Muslim-Croat entity of Bosnia.[37] The accords assumed that both entities would be multiethnic.[38] In practice, however, the Serb ambition for an ethnically nonmixed state might become the reality. This evolution toward de facto partition is primarily because Muslim or Croatian refugees from the rest of Europe are returning to new settlements in Bosnia, even if they were originally from the area now composing Republika Srpska. In addition, Serb refugees in Bosnia who are under Muslim or Croatian control will most likely be integrated into communities or new settlements in Republika Srpska.[39] The Western approach to resolving the Bosnian crisis has been to insist on a multiethnic state with some power sharing among various ethnic groups.[40] The Bosnian reality, however, has dictated a sharper division of the country along ethnic lines. The West finally capitulated to a watered-down version of the original Serbian position—a division of Bosnia according to ethnicity.

The Serb desire for a division along ethnic lines can be seen in an interview with the prime minister of the Republika Srpska:

We were interested in clearly defining our internal ethnic area on which we will make our Serbian state. . . . There are no conditions for life in common [in Bosnia-Hercegovina], or even for life next to each other. There have been so many sacrifices on both sides that it is impossible for wounds to heal so quickly and for both people to overcome what they have done to each other. This is the basic reason why I demanded that the area be divided once and for all time into a Serbian and Muslim part of Sarajevo.[41]

Following the Dayton Peace Agreement, Washington hoped that the Bosnian Croats, Muslims, and Serbs would adopt a vision of a unified country or at least a federation. A 1997 USIA poll, however, finds that these three ethnic groups still have divergent views. Before and after Dayton, Bosnian Serbs opposed a single Bosnia with near unanimity and Bosnian Muslims supported such an entity by similar margins. For the Bosnian Croats, moreover, opposition to a single Bosnia almost doubled after Dayton.

By an average of 94 percent across three USIA polls, Bosnian Serbs opposed a unified Bosnia. However, by an average of 98 percent, Bosnian Muslims took the opposite position. About a third of the Bosnian Croats polled supported a unified Bosnia at the time of Dayton, and about two-thirds were in opposition some seven months after Dayton in August 1996. As of January of 1997, the factions still had not come closer in their vision for a unified state. A survey conducted by the USIA found that 94 percent of the Serbs and 62 percent of the Croats continued to oppose a unified Bosnia. Only the Bosnian Muslims supported the unification by a margin of 98 percent.[42]

The other side of the coin to the opposition to a unified Bosnia is support for separate ethnic states. A USIA poll finds that the Bosnian Serbs and Croats are in basic agreement that, "every nation should have its own state." But with their emphasis on multiethnicity, the Bosnian Muslims strongly reject this idea of separateness. In 1996, a USIA poll found 84 percent of Bosnian Serbs and 76 percent of Bosnian Croats polled believe in ethnically separated states. Bosnian Muslims, however, reject this idea by a margin of 89 percent. A 1997 USIA poll found that 95 percent of Bosnian Serbs and 87 percent of Bosnian Croats believe that every "nation" should have its own state.[43]

The Dayton approach calmed the waters in Bosnia—at least temporarily. Meanwhile, the Western military presence in the region impedes military action by the former belligerents. Given the ethnic basis of internal political conflicts, the reaction of the parties once the external military deterrent power fades is of great import. The assumption here is that politicians use ethnic differences as a basis for acquiring and holding power. Given this tendency, the belligerents cannot be left to abide by the Dayton Peace Agreement on their own volition.

Just as Western interventionists choose to describe the events in the former Yugoslavia at the close of the 1980s from two different perspectives, so too do the national leaders themselves. Serbian leaders intent on using ethnicity for political purposes describe the conflict in Bosnia as a "civil war among ethnic groups." Bosnian Muslim leaders who wish to maximize outside intervention downplay ethnicity. They describe the conflict in Bosnia as an "international war among independent states." Over time, both descriptions are valid.

Prior to the disintegration of the Yugoslav state, the central authority in Belgrade represented by Marshal Tito, suppressed ethnic divisions. After Tito's death and the dissolution of the Soviet Union, Yugoslavia disintegrated into a series of "civil wars." But once the former republics declared their independence from Belgrade, their conflicts became an "international war." After NATO reinforced the ceasefire and began the implementation of Dayton, differences among the parties again became paramount. Hence, any interventionist solutions should take into account the enhanced salience of these differences.[44] Meanwhile, the virtual dance of Western diplomats made coercive diplomacy problematic at best.

CHAPTER FOUR

COERCIVE DIPLOMACY

INTRODUCTION

THIS CHAPTER ON COERCIVE DIPLOMACY defines this strategy as a combination of credible military power and diplomatic commitments in the process of coercion. While political hawks would use credible threats in order to compel actors to comply, doves would persuade them to comply via reassurance. A balanced policy would use threats when appropriate and reassurance when necessary.

The chapter considers the role of politics—both domestic American and alliance politics—as constraints on bargaining. Additionally, there is a detailed treatment of cases of attempted Western coercion in Bosnia: Sarajevo, Gorazde, and Bihac, as well as cases regarding the Serbian province of Kosovo.

Coercive diplomacy is a political military strategy that uses threats of future escalation or expansion of an ongoing war to achieve current diplomatic aims.[1] In contrast to brute force, which implies the destruction of an opponent, coercion is a process of inducing the adversary to choose compliance in order to avoid punishment. Coercive diplomacy suggests that a combination of force with diplomacy would be more effective than either diplomacy or force alone.

CLOSE WINDOWS OF OPPORTUNITY WITH POWER AND COMMITMENT

In the theory of coercive diplomacy, a core idea is that coercion might be successful if the target were acting to secure gains rather than to avoid losses. When prospective aggressors focus on possible gains, it is as if they are standing in front of windows of opportunity poised to act. Yet, because these opportunists concentrate on profiting, they also focus on limiting risk, reducing the likelihood of loss. Hence, when there is credible resistance from defenders, potential challengers may be deterred from incurring these costs.

When gain is the goal of challengers, they are risk-averse. When avoidance of loss is the aim, challengers are risk-acceptant. These two assumptions derive from prospect theory. A core idea of this theory is that people desire gains less than they fear losses. As a result, threats of sanctions are appropriate when people are in the domain of gain rather than in the realm of deprivation.

In other words, coercive diplomacy is only likely to be successful against actors in the domain of gain. At issue is how to determine the dominion for a particular actor. If the Bosnian Serbs planned to seize Bosnian Muslim heavy weapons from the UN-designated Sarajevo Exclusion Zone because of a desire for gain, they are good candidates for coercion. That is, the Bosnian Serbs should be unwilling to risk NATO airstrikes for the sake of acquiring someone else's weapons.

When possible attackers behave in order to maximize gains, they want to attain their goal but proceed cautiously in order to avoid negative consequences. They need to calculate carefully the risks of action and inaction. Coercive sanctions are relevant measures to confront such opportunists. Sanctions in this context are like "No Trespass" and "Warning" signs meant to deter crimes of opportunity. But just as there is a need to close windows of opportunity with power and commitment, there may be a need to open basements of fear with assurances.

OPEN DOORS TO BASEMENTS OF FEAR

When potential aggressors behave in order to avoid losses, it is as if they were trapped in a basement of fear. To escape the trap and avoid the loss, leaders are willing to take enormous risks. Threats of sanctions may be inappropriate for fearful individuals. Regardless of the likelihood of punishment, people who concentrate on avoiding expected losses tend to engage in risky behavior. To return to the Bosnia Serb example, if they were seeking to reacquire their own weapons from the exclusion zone, the Bosnian Serbs would be risk acceptant and less subject to NATO coercive threats.

If those in front of a window of opportunity are mercenaries, then actors in a basement of fear are paranoids. As a result of paranoia, they lack the ability to make cost-effective choices. Sanctions may even be counterproductive, leading to additional feelings of frustration, helplessness, and to further aggression.[2]

The process of escalation through miscalculation demonstrates the counterproductive aspects of threats when used in the context of interlocking fears. Prior to World War I, European nations were caught up in a mobilization race. Because of their fear of losing and their reluctance to face a resulting war few would have chosen to run this race. Mutual accommodation might have calmed their joint fears and perhaps avoided a war that not many actors wanted. The lesson coming out of World War I, however, was learned too well and misapplied to the events prior to the outbreak of World War II.

Due to fears of unintended escalation prior to the Second World War, the Allies incorrectly perceived how Hitler framed his situation. They assumed that he was in a basement of fear rather then a window of opportunity. They falsely believed that Hitler's motives and goals were limited and defensive rather than broad and offensive. In order to accommodate and appease him, the Allies sacrificed

Czechoslovakia, but appeasement was inappropriate. Hitler's goals were not limited only to Czechoslovakia. As a result of their miscalculation, the Allies found themselves in another world war.

HAWKS CLOSE WINDOWS OF OPPORTUNITY WITH CREDIBLE THREATS

The advice of political hawks is that leaders should, "close windows of opportunity with credible threats." In this respect, they advocate the use of coercive diplomacy, while minimizing the need to reassure.[3] Hawks favor policies designed to deter and coerce. In order to achieve conflict prevention, hawks would deter; in order to achieve conflict resolution on their own terms, they would coerce. Hawks assume that leaders accurately calculate the balance between gain and loss and that, as rational choosers, they weigh loss equally relative to gain. Hawks also assume that choosers act to maximize expected gain or minimize expected loss. According to hawks, calamitous situations, such as the 1991–1995 wars in the Balkans, are due to a vacuum of power and an absence of commitment.

Hawks presume that war results from the actions of power hungry, error-free, and coldhearted mercenaries who are not held in check by a combination of military capability and credible commitment. Hence, aggressors seek to exploit power and commitment vacuums. To avoid another situation like Bosnia in Kosovo, hawks might suggest a policy of "peace through strength and threat."

According to the hawks, leaders in Belgrade should be coerced from continuing to attack ethnic Albanian rebels in Kosovo. But coercion might be successful only if the Serbs perceive the expected costs to be greater than the anticipated gains from fighting. Irrespective of the threat of escalation in intensity and a geographical expansion of fighting, hawks would place a high premium on a predominance of NATO military capability and credible threats.

Through the eyes of hawks, the United States has two aims: that Serbia perceives that the costs of war outweigh the gains and realizes that the odds of losing are higher than the chances of winning.

Washington cannot assume that Belgrade understands this calculus. In order for Belgrade to be coerced to cease its attacks in Kosovo, Washington needs to make it very clear that the risks of going to war exceed the foreseen gains. Issuing credible threats to the regime's leaders is a surefire way to bolster deterrence and coerce successfully, according to the hawks.

World War II is the paradigm of the hawks: confront the Hitlers of the world to deter aggression or coerce them to cease fighting. World War I is a standard case for doves: reassure the threatened to avoid preemptive strikes and preventive wars.

DOVES OPEN BASEMENTS OF FEAR WITH REASSURANCE

The advice of political doves is that leaders should, "open basements of fear with reassurance." In this sense, doves would comfort the afflicted and reduce their frustration. Rather then using coercive diplomacy, doves would select accommodation and conciliation. In addition, doves would be attentive to the impact of commitment on potential escalation.

Hawks highlight the upside of explicit commitments—reinforcement of deterrence. Doves stress the downside of categorical commitments—unintended escalation. Commitments that are too precise may send the wrong signal to multiple audiences. Pledges to support the weaker side against its enemy may inadvertently prompt either side to take undesired or unforeseen action; the stronger actor might use this commitment as a rationale to take military steps against the weaker side.

American reluctance to support the proindependence movement in Kosovo serves as a prime example of a policy of "strategic ambiguity." If the rebels in Kosovo perceive an unambiguous NATO commitment to defend them, that might be a pretext for them to escalate their military action against the Serbian minority in Kosovo. Hence, NATO policy was consciously ambiguous: it implied a commitment to defend the ethnic-Albanian population in Kosovo without provoking Belgrade. Unlike hawks, doves are inclined to focus on such downside risks of commitments designed to reinforce deterrence.

Doves presume that threats to deter and coerce often provoke an already agitated leader to retaliate. This process drags all parties into an unwanted conflict. If there is a disastrous outcome, such as war, it would not be due to an interest vacuum or an absence of commitment. According to the doves, disaster results from the actions of fear-driven, mistake-ridden, risk-prone paranoids.

For doves, the main cause of any future war in the Balkans would be the destabilizing consequence of mutual efforts to reinforce deterrence or to engage in coercive diplomacy. Doves would perceive NATO threats as provoking an imperiled state like Serbia to risk preemptive attacks, preventive wars, or to escalate and expand ongoing combat.

According to doves, Western attempts to coerce Belgrade might unintentionally provoke Serbia to crack down on the ethnic Albanians of Kosovo. The Serbian leaders already believe that these Kosovars seek a Greater Albania that would include their Albanian kin presently living in places like Albania, Macedonia, and Serbia. For the doves, it is no surprise that Belgrade launched retaliatory attacks against the rebels. If Belgrade eliminated the vulnerable Kosovars, Serbia would be less subject to overwhelming Western military might. Doves would explain a Serbian decision to expand the fighting from Kosovo to rebel sanctuaries and supply lines along the Albanian-Kosovo border as a reaction to Western coercive diplomacy.

Doves extend the lesson of the First World War to the Balkans of the 1990s: reassure at all costs. Prior to the outbreak of World War I, Dual Alliance members (Germany and Austria-Hungary) and Triple Entente allies (England, France, and Russia) failed to reassure one another. As a result, alliance members saw efforts to reinforce deterrence as attempts to gain advantage. The principal European powers misjudged how their mobilization schemes would interact. Each feared that delay would allow its enemy to gain a decisive tactical advantage. They felt there was no choice but to escalate in order to avoid losing the advantage of going on the offensive. This perceptual security dilemma resulted in provocation and unintended war.

Both hawks and doves focus on the balance of power between challengers and status quo powers. For hawks, an imbalance in favor of the status quo actor should facilitate deterrence. For doves, a projection of imbalance in the long term may provoke a preventive war in the short term by the actor on the losing side of the trend. Hawks are globalists and believe that interventionists can dominate regional actors with military power followed by economic incentives. Doves take into account tribalism within regions; they are doubtful that outside power and economic incentives can determine outcomes in ethnic conflicts with ancient roots. Hawks assume that conflicts stem from rational choosers seeking current gains. Doves presume that conflicts derive from paranoids seeking to avoid losses based on ancient hatreds.

In light of this theoretical discussion of hawks and doves, consider American and Western efforts at conflict prevention and conflict resolution with respect to Serbia, Bosnian Serbs, and Kosovars, that is, ethnic Albanians in Kosovo. Following a treatment of American politics, there is a discussion of alliance politics. During 1991, at issue in the United States was how to prevent the outbreak of war as Yugoslavia disintegrated.

U.S. DOMESTIC POLITICS

Two approaches in the United States sought to answer the question of how to prevent war in Yugoslavia. American hawks preferred threats of force and military intervention if necessary. Doves in the United States believed that Yugoslavia was a European not an American problem, and that military intervention by outsiders would exacerbate ongoing ethnic disputes. Hawks were willing to try coercive diplomacy. They perceived potential aggressors as acting from windows of opportunity rather than from basements of fear.

The hawk of the hour during the 1992 presidential campaign was Governor Bill Clinton. He attacked President Bush for not being tough enough on the issue of Bosnia. The Clinton campaign held that the best chance to prevent war would have been to issue a credible warning that NATO airpower would be employed against any actor that dealt with the ethnic tensions in Yugoslavia with military means. Once the Clinton team took office, however, it was less inclined to issue threats. With responsibility of governance, the hawk of the hour became the dove of the day.

In spite of the president's waffling, other members of the administration favored a tough line on Bosnia; they included Vice President Al Gore, UN Ambassador Madeleine Albright, and Assistant to the President for National Security Affairs Anthony Lake. President Clinton and Secretary of State Warren Christopher initially took no clear position. But Secretary of Defense Les Aspin and his successor William Perry urged caution. While the president might have believed that ethnic cleansing was unacceptable, he did little to stop it. Rather, Clinton downplayed Bosnia as the administration focused on the American economy.[4]

Irrespective of bureaucratic differences, an understanding emerged in the American national security community around a policy of lifting the arms embargo on all the former republics of Yugoslavia and threatening NATO airstrikes—lift and strike. Recall that Serbia inherited heavy weapons from the arsenal of the former Yugoslavia, and Belgrade supplied the Bosnian Serbs with arms. In contrast, the Bosnian Muslims had no local arms supplier. Hence, Washington wanted to lift the embargo on all the former republics in order to permit arms to reach the Muslims.

The Clinton White House convinced a reluctant Pentagon bureaucracy to frame the Bosnian situation in terms of potential loss of NATO credibility in light of noncompliance by Belgrade. As a result, Washington was willing to run severe risks in order to deter and coerce Serbia. Britain and France, however, opposed the United States. Specifically, they were reluctant for NATO to adopt the lift and strike policy.

Although the alliance failed to lift the embargo, the allies began to look favorably on the deployment of troops for humanitarian purposes. And when economic sanctions alone did not compel the Serbs, peacekeeping provided an opening for the introduction of alliance airpower.

ALLIANCE POLITICS

Two key American allies were the United Kingdom and France, but London and Paris did not view the Bosnian situation as a top priority in post–Cold War Europe. Nevertheless, they agreed to deploy peacekeeping forces for humanitarian purposes rather than combat troops for coercive diplomacy or combat. Their aversion to the use of military force stemmed from a desire to minimize combat casualties and defense expenditures.

At first glance, it may appear that this aversion might have been because the British and French were in a domain of gain. Their unwillingness to use force, however, simply derived from the fact that Bosnia was not a priority for London or Paris. Because they had already risked their peacekeeping forces on the ground, they were reluctant to approve a large role for NATO airpower.

After considerable prodding from Washington, NATO decided in 1992 to use naval forces in the Adriatic Sea. A year later, the organization provided full authorization for the use of force to ensure compliance with UN demands that Serbia cease its combative role in the wars raging throughout the Balkans. On May 30, 1992, the Security Council adopted Resolution 757. It imposed economic sanctions on Serbia,[5] but these sanctions alone failed to result in compliance. On the same day the United Nations acted, President George Bush issued an executive order freezing Serbian assets and holdings held in the name of the former Yugoslavia. On June 5, 1992, Washington expanded its own sanctions to prohibit trade and other transactions.[6]

On October 16, 1992, NATO forces began to monitor flights in Bosnian airspace. The alliance took this action pursuant to the authorization of United Nations Security Council Resolution 781. Despite the ban on military flights in that airspace, the UN assessed that there were hundreds of flights that violated the prohibition between 1992 and 1993.

On March 31, 1993, UN Security Council Resolution 816 extended the ban to cover all flights not authorized by the UN Protection Force.[7] In the event of additional violations, Resolution 816 also authorized member states to take "all necessary measures," to ensure compliance with the ban. Acting under chapter 7 of the UN Charter, the "all necessary measures" phrase implies the use of military force. On April 8, 1993, the North Atlantic Council (NAC) authorized the enforcement of the UN ban.[8] The NAC also informed the United Nations of its willingness to undertake air operations pursuant to Resolution 816. NATO's Operation Deny Flight began on April 12, 1993 with France, the Netherlands, and the United States providing aircraft for the operation.

In light of this description of NATO preparations to use coercive diplomacy, consider specific actions taken around Sarajevo, Bihac, and Kosovo.

CONFLICT IN BOSNIA

Success of Sarajevo and Gorazde

Sarajevo. During the winter and spring of 1994, there were successful applications of coercive diplomacy around Sarajevo. On February 9, 1994, NATO demanded that the Bosnian Serbs remove heavy weapons from an exclusion zone or turn them over to UN control. The alliance coupled its demand with a threat of airstrikes. Assuming that the UN would request it, NATO authorized bombing raids against artillery or mortar positions in or around Sarajevo. The strikes were to be directed at Bosnian Serb positions from which there had been attacks against civilian targets in that city. As a result of the coordinated efforts of the UN and NATO during the February confrontation, the Bosnian Serbs withdrew their heavy weapons or placed them under UN control.

Gorazde. Another case where the NATO threat of force achieved diplomatic purposes began on or about April 10. At that time, UN Protection Force (UNPROFOR) military observers in the Bosnian City of Gorazde asked for NATO air cover. The UN Secretary General's special representative approved the request. Under the control of a UN forward air controller and acting under NATO command, two U.S. planes conducted bombing raids. The next day, the military observers made a second request for close air support in Gorazde. Again with the help of UN controllers, two additional American aircraft bombed selected targets.

Eight months before, August 3, 1993, NATO had identified threats to security around safe areas that would be grounds for airstrikes. By April 22, 1994, the alliance decided that the Bosnian Serb actions around the Gorazde safe area met conditions warranting bombing. At the request of the secretary general of the UN, NATO decided that the Bosnian Serbs should immediately cease attacks against the safe area, pull their forces back from the center of the city, and allow UNPROFOR free access to the area. NATO also declared a military exclusion zone around Gorazde and required all Bosnian Serb heavy weapons to be withdrawn by April 27. As a result of UN and NATO cooperation, and the selected airstrikes, there was effective compliance with the NATO ultimatums.

Because of repeated Bosnian Serb challenges to the Bosnian Muslims, the alliance encouraged the UN to take an additional diplomatic initiative, UN Security Council Resolution 836. The resolution calls upon member states to contribute forces to secure safe areas—places for Bosnian Muslims to live free from the destructive fire of the Bosnian Serbs.[9] The resolution authorizes member states, acting nationally or through regional organizations like NATO, to take "all necessary measures, through the use of air power, in and around the safe areas in the Republic of Bosnia and Herzegovina to support UNPROFOR in the performance of its mandate." The Bosnian Serbs, however, did not perceive United Nations authorization for NATO to take military action as a credible threat. In other words, coercive diplomacy failed, in June, 1994.

Following their refusal to be coerced, the Bosnian Serbs learned they could ignore UN and NATO warnings two months later. They disregarded a warning issued by the UN Protection Force on August 5, 1994. The Bosnian Serb army captured an arsenal of heavy armaments from a weapons storage site in the Sarajevo Exclusion Zone. As a result of the Bosnian Serb noncompliance, NATO launched airstrikes.

The Bosnian Serbs complied with UN demands after the NATO airstrikes. They returned the heavy armaments to the Sarajevo

Exclusion Zone. Because of their desire for gain, the Bosnian Serbs had taken heavy weapons from the zone. In the domain of gain, therefore, they were coercible. That is, the Bosnian Serbs were unwilling to risk NATO airstrikes for the sake of keeping these weapons.

Bankruptcy at Bihac

During October 1994, the Bosnian Muslim government authorized its army to launch an attack from Bihac to recapture its lost territory. Their victory proved to be a Pyrrhic one—the outcome was short-lived and resulted in escalation and expansion. That Bosnian Muslim policy was bankrupt: it gave the Bosnian Serbs a pretext to declare full-scale war against the Muslim forces.

In November 1994, about three thousand Croatian Serbs joined approximately ten thousand Bosnian Serbs to launch a counterattack against the Bosnian Muslims in Bihac. Around Sarajevo, Bosnian Serbs acted as if they were in a domain of gain and complied with UN and NATO demands. But around Bihac, the Bosnian Serbs acted as if they were in a domain of loss. Consequently, they were risk acceptant, and escalation ensued.

In response to the Bosnian Serb counterattack at Bihac, the United Nations Security Council took action on November 19, 1994. The council authorized NATO to strike targets in Croatia from where Serbs had launched attacks on Bihac. On November 20–21, NATO launched raids on the Udbina airfield in Serb-held Croatia. Although NATO succeeded in deterring further aircraft attacks from that part of Croatia controlled by the Serbs, the allies did not succeed in preventing the fighting around Bihac.

It was not a NATO policy of coercive diplomacy that failed at Bihac. Rather, the Bosnian Muslim regime had overextended itself, while it had simultaneously backed the Bosnian Serbs into a corner, and NATO did not threaten force in order to deter a Serb counterattack or compel a Serb withdrawal. Like the situation around Bihac, Kosovo offers another laboratory for testing whether coercive diplomacy failed or was not applied.

CONFLICT IN KOSOVO

Psychology and Kosovo

Three principles from psychology explain why it is difficult for NATO to coerce Serbia about Kosovo. The principles are loss aversion, the endowment effect, and effort justification. According to the principle of loss aversion, coercion is problematic if the target of pressure frames the situation in the domain of loss rather than gain. Recall that coercive diplomacy works best when the target frames a situation as one of gain.

Regarding the endowment effect, coercive diplomacy is less likely to be effective when individuals overvalue current possessions. People value what they have more than comparable items not in their possession. The very process of acquiring goods, moreover, enhances their value; that is, individuals endow their possessions with value in excess of what they paid for them originally.

With respect to effort justification, coercive diplomacy is doubtful if individuals overvalue as a result of the effort used to acquire the goods. The more effort it takes to obtain a set of goods, the more it is that individuals value those items. When loss aversion, endowment effect, and effort justification operate in the same direction, coercive diplomacy is of dubious validity.

Concerning Kosovo, Milosevic takes advantage of the fact that Serbs frame their situation in terms of loss aversion. Milosevic is a wily politician who manipulates mass fears for his own political gain. Because he has the support of a fear-driven Serbian population, it is difficult to coerce him about Kosovo. The endowment effect also affects the Serbian population. Kosovo's current value for the Serbs far exceeds its original cost. Because it has acquired increased value over time, it is doubtful that coercion will be effective for a long period. And regarding effort justification, the expenditure of Serbian blood and treasure in the acquisition of Kosovo gives it such a high value as to make effective coercion unlikely.

Given the centrality of the province to Serbian history, religion, and culture, losing Kosovo "is unthinkable" stated Warren

Zimmermann, American ambassador to Yugoslavia from 1989 to 1992. "While Bosnia was an adventure for Milosevic and the world recognized its independence," Zimmermann said, "it's much harder for Milosevic to make concessions in Kosovo, which is recognized as part of Yugoslavia."[10]

Bosnia is an adventure for Milosevic because it is not traditionally Serbian territory. As a result, Milosevic is in the domain of gain concerning Bosnia. Aspirations for a Greater Serbia include a land bridge connecting Serbs in Croatia and Bosnia with those in Serbia proper. Were he to launch a successful "adventure" with respect to Croatia and Bosnia, the outcomes would be gains, and Milosevic himself clearly would be in a domain of gain. In his desire to secure Bosnia for the Serbs who live there, consider Milosevic as a rational chooser, carefully weighing risks against gains. Because he is risk averse concerning Bosnia and Croatia, he was willing to negotiate in Dayton and make concessions about them.

Unlike Bosnia and Croatia, Serbs believe that Kosovo is their country. Serbs fear the loss of Kosovo more than they desire the gain of Bosnia. They are risk acceptant in order to keep what they had and have—Kosovo. Because Milosevic manipulates these fears, it is difficult but not impossible to coerce him not to use force to retain Kosovo.

Kosovo

With this theoretical analysis in mind, consider developments relating to Kosovo. The description divides into three parts—a period of Serb noncompliance (prior to October 1998), a time of comparative compliance (October–December 1998), and a phase of noncompliance (January–May 1999). At issue is why there is a transition from noncompliance to acquiescence and back to noncompliance. The assumption here is that the period of apparent submissiveness is a ploy on the part of Milosevic in order to persuade the West not to launch airstrikes or to continue its air war against Serbia.

Given the significance of Kosovo for all the parties, here is an overview of the important events. The years of 1389 and 1448 demarcate battles between Christendom and Islam in Kosovo. In 1389, the Orthodox Christian Serbs claim to have been defeated by the Turks intent on spreading Islam. In 1448, moreover, the Turks defeated the Roman Catholic Hungarians.

The battle of 1389, however, was not as forthright a failure for the Serbs as they would have others to believe. Indeed, the Serbian Empire had already dissolved about 30 years earlier, and the Serbian State remained on the scene for 70 years after the empire's demise. Irrespective of the facts, the Serbs perceive that they lost the battle for Kosovo, hence, Kosovo is to Serbs what Jerusalem is to Jews. Because of their defeat in 1389, the Serbs believed that Kosovo signified a lost opportunity. Having historically framed their situation concerning Kosovo in the domain of loss, Serbs are reluctant to comply with the demands of interventionist forces.

During the next centuries, ethnic Albanians immigrated to Kosovo, the Yugoslav constitution enshrined their autonomy in 1974, which created an autonomous province of Kosovo within the Serbian state. The longer the ethnic Albanians lived in Kosovo, the more they endowed Kosovo with value. This endowment effect makes it difficult for Kosovars—ethnic Albanians—to accept anything less than autonomy. In addition, poor living conditions in Kosovo during 1981 planted the seeds of a revolt by the ethnic Albanians against Serbian domination. Between 1989 and 1991, Slobodan Milosevic denied the autonomy that Marshal Tito had recognized, thus prompting the Kosovar secession struggle.

Washington versus Belgrade

Christmas Coercion. When the Kosovars began their struggle against Belgrade, President Bush sent his 1992 letter to President Milosevic, threatening the use of force in the event that Serbia launched an attack on Kosovo. On Christmas Day 1992, Bush warned Milosevic that violence against ethnic Albanians in Kosovo might lead to American military intervention. According to press accounts, Bush stated in a letter to Milosevic that in case of Serbian escalation in Kosovo, U.S. military force would be aimed at Serbian troops in that province as well as in Serbia itself.[11] Bush's letter to Milosevic signaled Washington's willingness to use force to back UN-authorized military operations. The goal was to prevent an expansion of fighting from Kosovo to neighboring states.

When Clinton took office in January 1993, he let the Bush threat stand. The warning "remained on the table," and "all options were open," in diplomatic parlance. But the Clinton administration was not able to persuade the allies to back up that threat with military action in Kosovo until the second Clinton term.

Holbrooke versus Milosevic.   While Washington's policies achieved some measure of success in Bosnia, Kosovo was more difficult. To obtain an accord at Dayton, the text of the agreement virtually ignored the conflict in Kosovo. In discussing the role Kosovo played at Dayton, Richard Holbrooke describes a discussion between himself and Milosevic:

> At Dayton, we had repeatedly emphasized to Milosevic the need to restore the rights of Kosovo's Albanian Muslims, which he had revoked when he absorbed the formerly autonomous province into Serbia. Our warnings at the time restrained him. But the long-feared crisis in Kosovo was postponed, not avoided.[12]

Holbrooke deserves praise for his success in taking the first step towards settlement of the Bosnian conflict instead of criticism for failing to settle the dispute over Kosovo. Nevertheless, ethnic Albanians took note of the fact that Dayton ignored their quest for autonomy and independence.

These ethnic Albanians—Kosovars—divided into two basic groups: doves led by Ibrahim Rugova, and hawks under divided rebel leadership. However, as fighting has occurred, the doves are becoming increasingly like the hawks. That is, the Kosovars' nonviolent demand for autonomy from Belgrade is giving way to a violent push for independence. Ignoring the doves and responding to the hawks, Milosevic launched a crackdown on the ethnic-Albanian majority in Kosovo during the spring and summer of 1998.

Ethnic-Albanian critics of the Clinton administration assert that it may have unintentionally facilitated a Serbian crackdown in Kosovo. They charge that the administration separated diplomacy from force, rather than reinforcing diplomatic initiatives with military threats. The critics cite the words of Holbrooke's colleague, American special envoy for the Balkans Robert Gelbard. During 1998, he praised Milosevic for cooperation in Bosnia and accused the rebel Kosovo Liberation Army (KLA) of being "a terrorist group." Not unexpectedly, Gelbard's statement sent shock waves through the ethnic-Albanian community of Kosovo. Gelbard was attempting to pursue an even-handed policy that sought to reinforce the limited cooperation coming from Belgrade, distance Washington from the violence of the KLA, and strengthen the hand of moderates among the ethnic-Albanian leadership.

The KLA compared Gelbard with former secretary of state Baker. During 1991, Baker had proposed that Yugoslavia remain a single entity. Milosevic interpreted Baker's proposal as a green light for Belgrade to move against Croatian separatists. Likewise, Kosovars perceived Gelbard's statement as a green light for Serbian military intervention in Kosovo.[13]

Critics also charge that Holbrooke reinforced Gelbard's conciliatory diplomacy toward Serbia. While Gelbard praised Belgrade and condemned the Kosovars, both American diplomats pressured the European allies to suspend sanctions on Serbia. An implicit promise of compliance by Belgrade almost resulted in the removal of sanctions. A move to impose sanctions, however, followed on the heels of this prior attempt to lift them.

The British and Germans believed that Milosevic had gotten the best of Holbrooke and Gelbard. These European detractors concluded that the wily Serb leader had "pocketed" an American concession without granting much in return. Milosevic pledged to open dialogue with political authorities in Kosovo but did not ensure that it would produce specific results. This promise of dialogue gave him diplomatic protection under which to launch a military crackdown on the rebels in Kosovo. The Serb president seemed to mix force with diplomacy, a formula that had been the specialty of the Americans. However, Holbrooke understood Milosevic's tactic. Holbrooke's promise to lift economic sanctions on Serbia was a rewarding carrot, while the sanctions themselves were a punishing stick. Holbrooke's effort to lift sanctions in proportion to Serb compliance was a

reasonable approach. Faced with a character like Milosevic, however, such reason was not as warranted as brute force.

Following the lead of Holbrooke and Gelbard, President Clinton's national security adviser also tried to use the promise of reward to induce Serb compliance. In discussing Kosovo during June
1998, adviser Samuel Berger said that American military intervention was "not on the table."[14] Later, however, U.S. officials said that
Berger really meant that unilateral American action was not being
considered because military planning would be left to NATO. Because of Berger's statement, there was need for a clarification that
would reinstitute the traditional American approach of combining
diplomacy with force; Washington attempted to marry American
diplomacy of rewards with the threat of NATO military action.

The executive branch effort aimed to enhance the prospect of
successful coercive diplomacy. That approach contrasted with con-
gressional actions that weakened U.S. credibility. Some members
gave the impression that Capitol Hill was pushing the Clinton administration to divorce force from diplomacy. Members of the Senate Armed Services Committee pressed special envoy Gelbard to set
a date for withdrawing American troops from Bosnia. Although
Washington favored an expeditious NATO study of military alternatives for Kosovo, Congress was not about to support any additional deployments. As some members of Congress were pressuring
the administration for a specific pullout date of American troops
from Bosnia, Congress was unlikely to favor ground force deployments in or near Kosovo.

It is ironic that American envoys favored lifting sanctions on
Belgrade, while European diplomats wanted to maintain these sanctions. Washington had a reputation of being tough on Milosevic;
European capitals have the "distinction" of being soft on Milosevic.
Indeed, European members of the Contact Group had been reluctant to adopt economic sanctions on Serbia in the first place. Once
implemented, however, the Europeans were also averse to lifting the
sanctions.

Bonn and London outflanked Washington with their tough
stance on Kosovo. The United Kingdom even worked in the European Union on behalf of sanctions against Serbia. In a meeting of

EU foreign ministers, London advocated reintroduction of the prohibition on new foreign investment in Serbia.

A ban on additional investment might hurt Serbia. Such a prohibition has the potential for drying up funds that Milosevic has used to finance the economy and thus to operate the country. An interdiction on outside investment might prevent foreign companies from taking part in sales of national firms. Milosevic had been using funds from such sales to underwrite his government.

Although there was little basis for their inference, the KLA interpreted American diplomatic statements as tacit consent from Washington for Serbian military intervention in Kosovo. The ethnic Albanians believed that American condemnation of the Kosovo Liberation Army along with the conciliatory rhetoric toward Serbia encouraged Belgrade to use force in Kosovo. The apparent division within the Clinton administration and the split between the United States and Europe lessened the likelihood of Serbian compliance with Western demands about Kosovo.

Doves versus Hawks in Kosovo. A gap in Kosovo between doves and hawks contributed to Serbian noncompliance. Milosevic had ignored the moderate leadership of Rugova but finally agreed to negotiations with the moderates by August 1998. But the Kosovar rebels declined to enter into the negotiations. By then, even the moderates became intemperate and demanded more than autonomy from Belgrade. Because the mandate of the August talks only included prospective autonomy rather than independence, the dissidents chose not to participate and the original moderates escalated their demands. Belgrade used the shift within the Kosovar community from the moderate to a hard-line position as a pretext to escalate hostilities.

Psychology Revisited

Recall the assertion from the Psychology and Kosovo section above that several reasons converged to undercut the prospects for coercing Serbia to cease its military intervention in Kosovo. The trio of psychological factors—loss aversion, endowment effect, and effort justification—explains why coercion was an unlikely outcome.

First, the Serbs had historically framed Kosovo as a domain of loss situation. Milosevic took advantage of this perceived loss for his domestic gain. Second, ancient memories over Kosovo increased its value. Third, the high price of battles fought caused the Serbs to overvalue Kosovo's worth. Acting together, these factors made coercive diplomacy a distant prospect, as may be seen in the following cases that evolved over 20 months, beginning October 1997. Belgrade intensified its challenge to the world community during October 1998, January/February 1999, and March/May 1999.

In the first case, October 1998, Milosevic escalated the fighting against ethnic Albanians in Kosovo, then apparently backed down by signing an accord negotiated by Holbrooke. The second case, January/February 1999, began with Milosevic violating that agreement. He again intensified Serbian assaults on the Kosovars but when faced with credible military power, he entered into diplomatic negotiations with his adversaries through members of the Contact Group. The third case, March–May 1999, is an extension of the second case, as the negotiations failed and hostilities commenced.

October 1998.   The fires that culminated in the confrontation of October 1998 actually began burning one year earlier. By mid-October 1997, the Kosovo Liberation Army had designated certain regions as restricted zones. As the Serbian police forces penetrated these areas, the KLA accordingly began to intensify its attacks on those forces. These raids resulted in sporadic combat between the KLA and Serbian armed units. As the casualties mounted, the ranks of moderate Kosovars decreased, and recruits to the more extreme KLA increased.

Tensions continued through the winter of 1998 when, in early February, Milosevic again sent troops into KLA-controlled areas. This action resulted in 80 Kosovar deaths, including the deaths of at least 30 women. Understandably, the angry Kosovars took to the streets of Pristina to protest the massacre. International condemnation of the hostilities was quick to follow. Washington criticized Belgrade as committing "terrorist actions." Although the United States continued to advocate unconditional negotiations, the massacre made such talks even more difficult than in the past. During the diplomatic stalemate, the international community took action. On

March 31, 1998, prompted by the continuing battles between the KLA and the Serbian police forces, the UN Security Council passed Resolution 1160, placing an arms embargo on the parties and calling for a peaceful, diplomatic end to their hostilities.

In early June, Milosevic again escalated hostilities, this time with the intention of eliminating the Kosovar threat to Serbia. The UN responded with the passage of Resolution 1174, which authorized member states to take "all necessary measures" to halt the fighting and restore peace and stability to the Balkan Peninsula. In this regard, the international community launched the Kosovo Diplomatic Observer Mission. As August arrived, the six nation Contact Group welcomed a statement from Milosevic that Belgrade would end the crackdown on ethnic Albanians. Again Milosevic was quick to break his promise when only two weeks later, the Serbian police force renewed its attacks on the ethnic Albanians.

While the fighting persisted, refugees continued to flee the province. By the third week in September, the United States and its allies began to coalesce around a common position. It was important for the Contact Group and the United Nations to be unified in their approach to Serbia. The UN Security Council demanded that Serbia end its offensive in Kosovo or confront international intervention. As the Contact Group prepared to meld the threat of force with previous diplomatic initiatives, the British and the French floated plans for another Security Council resolution. Their move resulted in the passage of Resolution 1199 on September 23, 1998.[15] Following the passage of this resolution, Washington issued another coercive threat that the NATO allies would be prepared to respond with force in the absence of diplomatic progress.

As the cold winter of 1998 loomed, NATO and the UN pushed for an agreement that required Serbian forces to withdraw from the Kosovo province under the watchful eye of international monitors. A major obstacle to such an agreement was Holbrooke's insistence that Milosevic agree to an expanded international monitoring mission by the Organization for Security and Cooperation in Europe that would verify compliance with the demands of the UN Security Council.[16]

With Holbrooke in Belgrade, United States secretary of state Madeline Albright continued to apply coercive measures. She held that Milosevic must comply with the long-standing political, humanitarian, and military demands of the international community or face the gravest consequences. In addition, Albright demanded that Serbia submit to international monitoring and verification of its compliance. Nevertheless, Milosevic continued to resist.

On October 16, 1998, in the midst of high-level negotiations between Holbrooke and Milosevic, NATO extended the deadline for Serbian withdrawal ten days. While the threat of force increased tensions, the extension of the deadline decreased threat credibility. Perhaps as a result of these mixed signals, the Holbrooke-Milosevic negotiations continued to yield no immediate agreement.

As the October 27 deadline approached, the allies prepared to launch a military attack. With the cruise missiles at the ready and planes on the runway, diplomacy on its last legs and force ready to carry the flag, Milosevic backed down. Holbrooke coerced the Serbian leader into compliance with the UN and NATO demands. However fleeting, this instance of coercive diplomacy succeeded. Because agreements with Milosevic tend to be transitory, Washington was quick to warn Belgrade again. The United States pledged to continue to pursue diplomacy combined with a credible threat of force. Indeed, rather than creating a peaceful long-term solution, the embers of the October agreement flared into burning hostilities at year's end.

January/February 1999. Milosevic's October concessions again proved empty, and Serb troop withdrawals, even under the guard of international verifiers, lost momentum. As the conflict rang in another year, fears of ethnic cleansing in the Kosovar province abounded. In the southern village of Racak, international monitors found the bodies of 45 ethnic Albanians, including three women and one young boy. Discovery of the massacre set off a critical chain of events. The American head of the international monitoring mission, William Walker, blamed the Serbs for the incident. Belgrade immediately threatened to expel Walker, and tensions mounted once again. In an uncharacteristic display of toughness, UN secretary general Kofi Annan insisted that the time to use force was drawing near. Even Paris saw the need to reinforce the threats that were on the table. French diplomats asserted that in the absence of the use of force to back NATO diplomacy, the allies might risk even greater damage to the credibility of their commitment to peace.

The Contact Group met on January 28, 1999 to discuss plans for military action against Serbia. Following that meeting, Albright continued to press for coercive diplomacy as a means of effecting Serbian compliance to the demands of the international community. Indeed, the American approach was to seek diplomatic goals backed by the threat of force. The aims were that both sides halt the violence and come immediately to the negotiating table.

Whether the combination of threats and diplomacy would be effective would soon be clear. On January 30, 1999, two days following the Contact Group meeting, international monitors discovered a mass grave of 24 ethnic Albanians in the City of Rugova. After a series of charges and countercharges regarding responsibility for the massacre, the allies threatened to use force unless the parties attempted to resolve their differences. Just before the bombing was to commence, Belgrade agreed to send a delegation to the all-party talks in Rambouillet, France.

The Contact Group plan of January 1999 was derived from the October 1998 cease-fire, negotiated between Milosevic and Holbrooke. It had three basic elements. The first promised autonomy for the Kosovars. The second demanded that Belgrade withdraw all of its security forces from Kosovo, Serbian paramilitary police units in particular. The third called for disarmament of the KLA fighters. Some of them had hoped to be reemployed as law enforcement personnel in the autonomous part of Kosovo. Regarding autonomy, the plan offered ethnic Albanians local control of the legislature, police, and the judiciary.

Kosovo was to remain a part of Serbia for at least three years, rather than the independence favored by the KLA. After that transition period, there would be a review of its final status. The ethnic Albanians preferred to have a referendum to determine whether there would be independence for Kosovo. There was an assumption on the part of the Contact Group members that the KLA would accept the January plan, which did not include a referendum. In fact, however, neither the KLA nor Belgrade agreed to the plan during February 1999 talks in France. Even if the local parties eventually adopt the plan, acceptance does not mean that they would comply with its terms. And in the event of noncompliance, at issue is whether steps should be taken to compel the parties to implement the terms of the agreement.

March-May 1999. A seamless web connects the timelines between the January/February and March–May cases. On February 7, 1999, the Kosovo peace talks opened in Rambouillet, a diplomatic stalemate ensued, and Western mediators called for a new round of talks in three weeks. Also on February 19, the second round of negotiations broke down, and Belgrade rejected the Rambouillet proposal. Washington warned that NATO was planning airstrikes against Serb military forces. In spite of the warning, Belgrade cracked down on villages in Kosovo.

On March 24, NATO launched a series of airstrikes on Serb forces, with the goal of stopping the Serb military offensive. Human rights groups expressed the fear that hostilities would exacerbate the Serb assault on civilians and accelerate their flight from Kosovo. Not only did round-the-clock NATO airstrikes fail to coerce Belgrade, but also they had unintended effects. The strikes intensified a Serb crackdown on ethnic Albanians that was already underway and thus indirectly hastened their exodus from Kosovo. By April 19, after over 6,000 allied sorties (a mission flown by a single plane in a given day) during the first four weeks of hostilities in the spring of 1999, NATO had not stopped the Serb offensive. Indeed, at the beginning of airstrikes on March 24, Belgrade had about 36,000 troops in and around Kosovo; within a month, however, there were some 43,000 troops.

On April 6, Milosevic announced a unilateral ceasefire, but NATO rejected the offer as disingenuous. A week later Serb forces expanded the war into northern Albania, provoking a warning from Washington that Serbia should refrain from attacking neighboring countries.

At issue is the nature of the miscalculations that led to the escalation of hostilities. Faulty intelligence and faulty policy analysis resulted in miscalculated escalation.

The main interagency document of the intelligence community is a National Intelligence Estimate (NIE). A November 1998 estimate concluded that Milosevic was susceptible to outside pressure. As long as he retained power, he was vulnerable to NATO threats. And a January 1999 NIE determined that Milosevic did not want a war he could not win. After maintaining his honor with resistance, the NIE held that he would rapidly comply with NATO demands. Finally on March 24, a special NIE concluded that Milosevic would cease his crackdown on ethnic Albanians and comply with the terms of Rambouillet if he suffered or anticipated experiencing significant damage to the Serb military and national infrastructure from NATO airstrikes.

Optimistic intelligence estimates reinforced worldviews of policymakers. Hawks in Washington described Milosevic as "a schoolyard bully who would back down after one good punch on the nose." This image of Milosevic implies that he is in a domain of gain and hence would be risk-averse in circumstances in which he confronts credible threats. Although this image may be a necessary one for Milosevic in Bosnia, he utilizes Serb sense of loss regarding Kosovo as a means of bolstering his own domestic political position. In short, the bully image applies to the Milosevic of Bosnia; it does not apply to the Milosevic of Kosovo.

Recall that Slobodan Milosevic came to power as a result of defending the Serb minority in Kosovo against ethnic Albanians. He fears that any compromises on Kosovo might threaten his hold on power in Belgrade. Because Milosevic is in a domain of political loss regarding the province, he is risk-acceptant with respect to NATO airstrikes. And the Serb people are in a domain of cultural loss with respect to Kosovo, due to important Eastern Orthodox Christian religious sites in that province. Because coercive diplomacy is at best problematic and at worst counterproductive when the target is in a domain of loss, NATO failed to coerce Milosevic to comply with its demands. At issue are what steps NATO should take when confronting noncomplying actors like

Milosevic, as evidenced in the March–May 1999 failure of coercive diplomacy over Kosovo.

After Detection, What?

Factors that underlie the enforcement of diplomatic agreements by outside actors include: inspecting to ascertain compliance by parties to an accord, determining which side is in violation of the agreement, and deciding whether to react in event of noncompliance given the goals of external actors toward the local parties. Here is a statement of these factors as general principles.

First, international actors should seek to regulate only that which can be monitored; in addition, there must be clear violations of an accord by one side before such regulations can be enforced. Second, the technique for ensuring compliance should be compatible with the set of objectives that international enforcers have in relation to local actors. Third, there should be an understanding among the enforcers about the level of noncompliance that would trigger what range of retaliation.

To illustrate these three principles in the case of Kosovo, consider the sequence of agreement, detection of noncompliance, and the difficulty the international community had in fashioning a policy of retaliation. With respect to the October 1998 ceasefire and its January 1999 plan for Kosovo, aircraft and onsite inspectors were able to monitor the objects of regulation. Given the inability of UN economic sanctions to compel the regime in Belgrade, interventionists chose the threat of NATO military force as the method to address noncompliance. This method was incompatible with objectives, however: the use of force might have endangered progress toward an overall settlement between Serbia and the Kosovars in peace talks held in France during February and March 1999.

Both Belgrade and the KLA had made repeated violations of the October 1998 pullback accord negotiated between Milosevic and Holbrooke. However, in March 1999, Belgrade massed Serbian forces along the Kosovo and Macedonia borders, increased the number of paramilitary police officers in Kosovo, launched attacks against the KLA, and deployed heavy weapons near that province. Under the terms of the accord with Holbrooke, Milosevic agreed to maintain a ceasefire, refrain from massing troops, limit the number of paramilitary officers, and restrict the size of weapons in the area. Although these were clear violations of the terms of the October agreement, there was little consensus within NATO on the "trigger" that would justify retaliatory airstrikes. A pre-agreed level of violation that would activate a NATO response had not been established.

Credibility Gap?

The reluctance of NATO to use force against Serbia gave rise to charges of a credibility gap. Threats not backed up with force lead to a diminution of the credibility of NATO threats for future situations. The alliance set a number of deadlines that did not produce compliance. Rather than using force, however, the allies extended the deadlines. February 20 and 23, 1999 were two such deadlines.

Critics complain that there was a serious erosion of Western credibility as a result of setting deadlines without effect and a lack of force in the face of noncompliance. They charge that making threats that others ignore exposes NATO and the United States particularly as a "paper tiger" only willing to engage in "bluff and bluster." Issuance of ultimatums places NATO in a corner from which the only way out is an "ill-advised use of force."[17] Critics label the Clinton Administration's Kosovo policy as "moralistic bluster followed by hesitancy and inaction."[18]

Loss of credibility, however, is not the only issue underlying the dispute between critics and NATO. Rather, at issue is whether NATO in general and the United States in particular should engage in peacemaking in places like Bosnia and Kosovo.

CONCLUSIONS

International efforts to coerce Bosnian Serbs to cease their attacks against the Bosnian Muslims and to prevent Serbia from oppressing the Kosovars illustrate theoretical ideas about coercive diplomacy.

The UN and NATO were successful when they closed Serbian windows of opportunity with power and commitment. Securing compliance around Sarajevo and Gorazde highlights when coercion is likely to be successful. When Bosnian Serbs acted on the basis of gain and were vulnerable to international airstrikes, compliance was forthcoming.

The UN and NATO were less successful in securing Bosnian Serb acquiescence around Bihac. When Bosnian Serbs acted from anxiety in the Bihac area, they were not subject to international coercion. Because they were in a basement of fear, brute force rather than coercive diplomacy was the only viable option.

Also, consider the Bosnian Muslim decision to risk civilian casualties for the benefit they expected to gain by continuing to fight the Bosnian Serbs. The Muslim leadership valued the self-determination of a sovereign multiethnic state over the safety of its civilian population. Self-determination was the expected gain of noncompliance for the Bosnian Muslims. It outweighed the expected loss—Serbian attacks against the Muslim population in Sarajevo, Gorazde, and Bihac.

With respect to Kosovo, Serbs framed their situation as one of loss rather than gain. Milosevic took advantage of this framing in order to take a hard line against NATO intervention. Thus, it was difficult to apply coercive diplomacy to compel Serbian attacks against the rebel Kosovars.

Another reason why coercive diplomacy was more successful for Bosnia but problematic for Kosovo concerns the degree of leverage available to interventionists. In contrast to Bosnia, the UN and NATO lack influence over the parties in the conflict over Kosovo. Expatriate Albanians in the former Yugoslav Republic of Macedonia and the Yugoslav Republic of Montenegro raise money for their ethnic kin to purchase weapons and smuggle them into Kosovo across porous borders from neighboring entities. And if the KLA begins to lose its war with the Serbs and civilian casualties mount, it expects NATO airstrikes against Serbia irrespective of whether the KLA accepts the Contact Group plan that promises only autonomy rather than statehood for Kosovo.

Interventionists also lack influence over Serbia. The main leverage of the outsiders includes economic sanctions and threats of cruise missile attacks from sea-based platforms or from warplanes. These tools would have to be supplemented by NATO ground combat troops in order to provide a credible threat to Belgrade. But, people neither live on the sea nor in the air; they live on the land! Hence, ground combat units are inherently more credible than sea- or air-based units. And by discussing an international ground force presence only in the context of a peace accord among the warring parties, the threat credibility drops precipitately.

What are lessons learned from the Kosovo cases? First is the major theme of this chapter: when political and military tracks move in tandem, they reinforce each other. Second, there is a need for external parties to be unified in their approach lest regional actors use disunity as a pretext for failure to comply with the demands of the interventionists.

Prior to reaching consensus about the efficacy of combining force with diplomacy, France and Germany worried that NATO airstrikes might be fruitless and even intensify the conflict. Led by Paris and Bonn, European diplomats had been reluctant to make threats of military action. They believed such strikes might inadvertently encourage the Kosovo Liberation Army to assume that Western planes were providing tactical air support for KLA ground operations.

A common position in NATO emerged in part because Moscow ceased objecting to the idea of merging the diplomatic and military tracks. In addition to Russian noninterference, the United Nations contributed to the emergence of the NATO plan. UN secretary general Kofi Annan told NATO that the threat of force was necessary to allow diplomacy to bring peace to Kosovo.

A third lesson learned from the Kosovo cases concerns Belgrade's strategy of initial compliance with international requirements but subsequent noncompliance. With respect to UN and NATO demands for withdrawal of Serbian forces, the Serbian stratagem is to feign compliance in order to buy time in the hope and expectation that the international community will tire of coercing compliance.

A fourth lesson involves the authority by which international institutions intervene in the domestic affairs of a sovereign state.

One of the reasons why Serbia is reluctant to comply fully with NATO demands is because Belgrade views Kosovo as an integral part of Serbia. At issue is the legitimacy of NATO military intervention in Kosovo, which is part of a sovereign Serbian territory.

A principal justification for intervention is Article 3 of the Fourth Geneva Convention, which applies to conflict not of international character, such as the situation in Kosovo. The article states that people taking no active part in hostilities shall be treated humanely, without any adverse distinction based upon race, color, religion or faith, birth, or wealth. The article bans humiliating and degrading treatment as well as violence to life and person. In particular, the article prohibits murder of any kind, mutilation, cruel treatment, and torture. Because of their ethnic identity, Belgrade drove over 200,000 Kosovars from their homes even before the March–May 1999 hostilities between NATO and Serbia.

A fifth lesson of the Kosovo cases concerns the necessity that diplomats have finite goals and to pursue them with credible means. NATO limited its goals in Kosovo and threatened military action to achieve them. By so doing, the organization improved the likelihood of gaining some compliance from Belgrade. NATO called for an end to the Serbian crackdown on ethnic Albanians but did not advocate independence for them. In particular, Washington explicitly did not support independence for Kosovo. The United States wanted "Serbia out of Kosovo, not Kosovo out of Serbia."[19]

While bounded aims helped persuade Belgrade to accept a deal, such finite purposes were insufficient to induce the Kosovars to accept that arrangement in the January/February 1999 talks. Once at the table during the winter 1999 negotiations in France, a gap appeared between NATO goals and the means for achieving them. As a result of that breach, it became very difficult for coercive diplomacy to succeed in Kosovo.

Because Serbia did not perceive Western threats as credible, Belgrade imagined that it could engage in cost-free suppression of ethnic Albanians. In this respect, coercive diplomacy was unlikely to be effective, and brute force became the option of choice. Rather than a mix of threat and promise to achieve diplomatic purposes, a strategy of brute force would simply bomb the adversary. Defenders would use force for the sake of degrading challengers' capabilities rather affecting their motivations and intentions, as is the purpose of coercive diplomacy.

In the bureaucratic politics of American decisionmaking, political hawks seem to be vindicated in Bosnia: threats and force generally deterred and coerced successfully. Doves find solace in Kosovo: threats and force for the most part failed to deter and coerce, leaving only brute force as the means of achieving Western objectives.

Bosnia suggests the utility of a rational choice framework. Kosovo highlights the usefulness of prospect theory as a valid explanation of events defined by historical circumstance.

CHAPTER FIVE

CIRCUMSTANCE AND CHOICE

PHILOSOPHIES OF CONFLICT

As stated earlier, analysts often employ two approaches to explain political events: circumstance and choice. In literature, they correspond to the writings of Marx and Freud on the one hand, versus Dostoyevski and Machiavelli on the other hand.

Marx believed that unjust institutions explain why individuals engage in antisocial behavior. In the *Communist Manifesto,* Marx calls for the elimination of the institution of private property. Destroying this institution, he argues, would free the proletariat from a need to engage in class struggle with the bourgeoisie. Historical circumstance does the heavy lifting in Marxian explanations. With respect to Kosovo, a Marxist-like interpretation is that "ancient hatreds" explain current policymaking.

Dostoyevski holds that individuals take part in iniquitous behavior because they seek advantage. Post facto justifications abound in order to rationalize antisocial behavior. In Dostoyevski's *Crime and Punishment,* Raskolnikov justifies the murder of the pawnbroker. But at the end of the day, he confesses to his evil deed as a matter of conscious decision. Rational choice is the main explanation in Dostoyevskian logic.

Like Marx's emphasis on historical circumstance, Freud's emphasis on bad experiences in childhood uses early background circumstances to explain later problems in adults. According to Freud's theory of psychoanalysis, childhood history might explain why people are aggressive in adult life. When Freud heard patients' reports of depression, nervousness, and obsessive habits, he became convinced that their symptoms had mental not bodily causes. Patient distress was a result of conflicts, memories, and emotional traumas that occurred in childhood.

From the perspective of circumstance, present political problems in the Balkans can be attributed to political paranoia acquired through negative historical memories. Hence, a primary justification for the current tensions in the former Yugoslavia is that different ethnic groups lost portions of their land at different times in history. At stake in Kosovo is how to weigh Serbian legalities and group memories against Albanian demographics and collective memories. Because Kosovo is a current province of Serbia, Belgrade has an internationally recognized legal claim over Kosovo. In addition, Serbs have historical roots in the province and an obsessive fear of losing the land that is home to ancient battlefields and longstanding monasteries of their Orthodox faith.

Although about 90 percent of the populace was ethnic Albanian during the 1990s, the Serbs still regard Kosovo as their own. But Serbian memories and fears have little salience to the ethnic Albanians who reside in Kosovo. They also have collective memories of the same land, but to them it is a part of a Greater Albania dream not a Greater Serbia nightmare. Hence, in accordance with the argument that focuses on circumstance, ancient hatreds are the root of collision.[1]

In connection with the approach that emphasizes choice, current political problems in the Balkans are due to the conscious decisions of politicians seeking advantage. Thus, a main explanation for the present conflict is that Machiavellian leaders use ethnicity as a pretext for political gain. Instead of historical circumstance being the ultimate determining factor in political decisionmaking, rational choices made by individual "princes" determine policy. According to the choice model, historical events may play into policy decisions, but the ultimate responsibility lies on the shoulders of leaders who make choices.

However, neither circumstance nor choice fully explains political behavior. Rather, both circumstance and choice combine for a complete explanation. The first camp, circumstance, explains why it is difficult to resolve ethnic conflicts. Such conflicts derive from the circumstance of heterogeneous populations, and behavior derives from fear rather than gain. The second camp, choice, explains why conflict resolution is possible. The conflicts stem from autocratic leaders whose behavior derives from gain. Although memories are difficult to erase, leaders are expendable: they can be changed. When politicians make use of ethnic heterogeneity for domestic gain, they exacerbate latent problems and hence threaten international peace and security.

HETEROGENEITY

Actors in situations like the Balkans are highly heterogeneous. The Bosnian Croats, Muslims, and Serbs as well as the Kosovars are divergent in their attributes and views. Moreover, the overall entity—Bosnia—is almost a "failed state." As a platform for negotiation, a failed state is virtually a nonentity. It is a state in name only, neither able to provide security against external threats, nor able to ensure domestic tranquility. An example of a failed state is Somalia during the 1990s. As the twentieth century closes, Bosnia has not become a Somalia. Although there are differences in level of development between a European country like Bosnia and an African nation like Somalia, the recurrence of war might lead Bosnia to go the way of Somalia.

Conflict among heterogeneous groups in the Balkans takes place at a subnational level. At this level, minority groups command greater attention than their actual numbers warrant. These minorities include Croats residing in the Republika Srpska and the Serbs living in the Muslim-Croat entity of Bosnia. The interaction of minority populations with majority populations complicates outside efforts at intervention.

In Kosovo, a Serb minority of about 10 percent governs the majority Kosovars. Macedonian Albanians make up over 20 percent of that country's population and tend to identify with other ethnic Albanians across the frontier: these brethren reside mainly in northeastern Macedonia, which borders Kosovo, a province with a 90 percent ethnic Albanian population. Consider the significance of these percentages. As the proportion of minorities within majority areas increases, so too does the number of concerns and demands that have to be accommodated. A temporary alternative to the voluntary reconciliation of competing ethnic groups is coercive diplomacy. A long-term option is commercial diplomacy. Meanwhile, it is necessary for U.S. military power to cast a long political shadow across the Atlantic.

American power brought the Croats, Muslims, and Serbs of Bosnia to the table and temporarily synchronized their conflicting requirements. But eventually there has to be an accommodation based upon a resolution of the opposing demands. Although "ancient hatreds" constrain conflict resolution, heterogeneity alone is not an insurmountable barrier. However, ethnic animosities reinforced by fear-driven paranoids make conflict resolution less likely.

FEAR

Weak groups involved in interethnic conflicts act as if they were in a "basement of fear." In the basement, militarily feeble groups risk the consequences of noncompliance in order to avoid losses. Having lost their homes to Croats, Bosnian Serbs of the Krajina region of Croatia would give greater weight to potential losses than to prospective gains. Serbs in Kosovo also fear losing ancient lands to ethnic Albanians. For the Serbs of Kosovo, future losses are more salient than anticipated gains.

Likewise, ethnic Albanians have their own fears. They dread losing their homes to interlopers, whose ancient claims are suspect at best. When Croatia ousted the Serbs from the Krajina, Belgrade sent some of them to Kosovo. The aim was to increase the Serbian proportion of the population. Immigration of Croatian Serbs to Kosovo only served to increase the fears of the ethnic Albanians.

As a result of interacting fears, rational action is rare.[2] The actors give unreasonable justifications for their failure to comply with demands that they cease hostilities. They continue to fight despite outside efforts to make peace. They use ceasefires not as down payments on a permanent settlement, but as occasions for recuperation and rearmament.

According to a United States Information Agency poll taken in January 1997, Bosnian Serbs and Croats strongly agree with the following idea: "People can feel completely safe only when they are the majority nationality in their country." By margins of over 90 percent, both groups favored separateness. While the margins among the Bosnian Muslims are much less, approximately half also prefer segregation to integration. These statistics are up from a poll conducted in June of 1996 finding 84 percent of Bosnian Serbs, 86 percent of Croats, and 43 percent of the Bosnian Muslims in agreement with this sentiment.[3] Thus, the Bosnian Serbs, as well as Croat and Muslim forces in Bosnia are so fearful of losing their ethnic identity that they take extraordinary chances in resisting the implementation of the Dayton Peace Agreement.

Additionally, Bosnian Croat and Serb leaders are afraid that their prior human rights sins are coming home to haunt them in the form of indictments from the International Criminal Tribunal in The Hague. Article 146 of the Fourth Geneva Convention of 1949 on the Protection of Civilian Persons in Time of War calls for penal sanction of those committing or ordering to commit "grave breaches" of the convention; and the search for such persons to be brought to trial. As of November 1997, the War Crimes Tribunal at The Hague indicted 78 suspects: 18 Bosnian Croats (23 percent), three Bosnian Muslims (four percent), 51 Bosnian Serbs (65 percent), three of unknown ethnic background (four percent), and three Serbian officers from the former Yugoslav People's Army (four percent). They were charged with involvement in genocide and crimes against humanity. Twelve suspects have been apprehended with 10 suspects being held in custody at The Hague.[4]

The most conspicuous and potentially detrimental aspect of a fear-driven motivation is "ethnic outbidding." This term refers to the process whereby ethnic group leaders attempt to outbid one another in their hard-line stances. Ethnic outbidding combines circumstance and choice. Politicians use fear to gain advantage.

According to the school of thought that emphasizes circumstance, fear motivates politicians. Afraid of appearing weak, they miss windows of opportunity for accommodation and reconciliation. Such was the case in 1993 when the leaders of Serbia, Croatia, and Bosnia, including Bosnian Serb and Croat leaders came to the table to discuss a settlement through the Vance-Owen Peace Plan. According to the stipulations of that approach, Serbia had to give up territories it acquired by force and "ethnic cleansing." Nonetheless, Belgrade and its Bosnian Serb allies would have retained approximately 43 percent of Bosnian territory.[5]

The Bosnian Serb parliament rejected Vance-Owen, in order to retain their control over 70 percent of Bosnia-Herzegovina.[6] In April of 1993, the revised peace plan met the same fate. While Karadzic finally signed the Vance-Owen Peace Plan in May of that year, he was not supported by the parliament of the Serbian Republic of Bosnia. Instead, the parliament called for a referendum to be conducted among the Bosnian Serb population. The May referendum found the Vance-Owen Peace Plan unacceptable to the Bosnian Serbs by a margin of 96 percent.[7]

In light of the military advantage enjoyed by the Bosnian Serbs, the approval of Vance-Owen might have been perceived as a sign of weakness. Hence, there was a missed opportunity for reconciliation among the parties. In such a case, conflict escalates rather than diminishes. Because none of the actors wanted to appear weak, prospects for accommodation languished.

Consequently, ethnic outbidding among leaders created greater divisions among their followers as "nationalism" spread from the top, down. Just as the Croatian president, Tudjman, stated that he was grateful his wife was neither a Serb nor a Jew, one Croat follower similarly expressed his abhorrence for Serbs, whom he refers to as "Chetniks."

> Serbia is a . . . little landlocked country of absolutely no value, populated by an uncivilized, uncultured and demented "people." . . . If anyone should be getting revenge, it should be the

Croatians and the Muslims for all the hundreds of thousands of Croatians and Muslims that you bastards murdered in World War II and in the current war. If I had it my way I would have all the Chetniks rounded up and shot . . . You Chetniks make me sick.[8]

In short, ethnic outbidding in the Balkans abounds. There is a premium placed on ethnic leaders who can be the most virulently opposed to other factions. A consequence of fear-driven motivation is misperception.

MISPERCEPTION

Before Dayton, misperception was rife between outside negotiators and ethnic insiders. Because of distorted information, conflict resolution became less likely. Motivated and unmotivated biases resulted in misperception. When individuals see what they want to see, that is an example of a motivated bias that leads to misperception. When people see what they expect to see, that is an example of an unmotivated bias that also distorts perception.[9]

On the motivated side, the Germans favored the Croatians and the Russians preferred the Serbs. Therefore, these Contact Group members "saw what they wanted to see," when viewing the activities of the Croats and Serbs, respectively. Bonn and Moscow had motivations that distorted their perception. Similarly, the Americans did not want to see trouble in the Balkans that would have increased pressure for an unpopular intervention. Because the United States was in the middle of national elections, President Bush did not want to perceive a war-torn Bosnia. Such a perception would have created pressure for American military intervention.

On the unmotivated side, the allies viewed the Balkans as an arena of historic instability. This expectation caused them to downplay conflict in Bosnia at any given time. As a result, the allies discounted Serbian actions that suggested an intention to take over the whole of Bosnia. Indeed, both unmotivated expectations and motivated preferences converged. As a result, the allies discounted Serbian aggressive behavior. Misperception abounded between outside

negotiators and ethnic insiders. And because of distorted information, conflict resolution became more difficult.

Illustrative of an unmotivated bias on perception is a statement
by secretary of state Albright concerning President Milosevic. She said
that, "I don't think Mr. Milosevic has perfect pitch in what he hears,
I hope very much that he will understand and get the message."[10] Because of a lack of follow through on prior warnings, Milosevic
doubted the credibility of current threats. Hence, he did not listen to
the message that Albright wanted him to hear: comply with American
demands and cease military intervention in Kosovo.

While heterogeneity, fear, and misperceptions complicate outside efforts to resolve internal conflicts, another factor concerns the
tendency for ethnic leaders to rule in a dictatorial fashion. The second school of thought, choice, provides a complementary explanation of constraints on conflict resolution. In this respect, conflicts
stem from autocratic leaders whose behavior derives from gain.

AUTOCRACY

Actors of an autocratic nature often dominate ethnic conflicts. By
definition, authoritarian leaders have little regard for democratic
methods for resolving multiparty conflict. But diplomatic interventionists, such as the Contact Group for Bosnia, often come from
countries steeped in democratic traditions. Outside peacemakers
from representative democracies have little knowledge of how to
cope with Machiavellian warlords and rogue leaders. While bargaining and compromise are integral elements of Western order,
they are rare in Balkan disorder.

Dayton was a watershed event in that it facilitated a major
change in bargaining practices among the ethnic groups. By compelling a time out and imposing a peace process, Dayton allowed
new modes of bargaining to emerge. The hope was that the parties
would learn to bargain with one another under the protection and
tutelage of the interventionists.

In addition to the bargaining gap between the Contact Group
and the actors in Bosnia and Kosovo, there is a fault line between

activist leaders and their more passive followers. What ethnic elites want for their group is bound to be self-serving. It is no surprise that rogue leaders exacerbate hostilities in order to shore up their own power bases. Recall that Serb leader Milosevic stoked the fires of latent nationalism to secure his presidency.

Consider how Milosevic took advantage of anti-Albanian sentiment among the Serbs in order to enhance his political power in Belgrade. Serbs living in the autonomous province of Kosovo found themselves dominated by the ethnic-Albanian majority population. When local police attacked a crowd of demonstrating Serbs in 1988, Milosevic appeared on the scene as a leader of the Serbs against Albanian domination.

In order to eliminate Albanian control, Milosevic wanted to place Kosovo under the jurisdiction of the Serbian Republic. He also mobilized one ethnic group against the other. Milosevic rallied nationalist Serbs against Albanian men whom he alleged had raped Serbian women en masse.[11] Portraying the largely undocumented rapes as an attack on the Serb nation and culture, Milosevic successfully played the ethnic card. Hence, he mobilized political support for himself.

Interethnic conflict served the function of reinforcing intraethnic political strength. Conflict between ethnic Albanians and Serbs was a point of departure for boosting political fortunes within the Serbian group. It is no surprise that ethnic outbidding is a product of the need to reinforce the political power bases of ethnic group leaders. By retaining a common outside foe, leaders also enhance their inside political positions.

Milosevic is not alone in exacerbating out-group tensions for ingroup benefits. President Tudjman of Croatia also secured his power base by mustering antagonism against the Serbs. In addition, he used military force against the Serbs in Croatia, "Operation Storm," for his own domestic political gain. During August 1995, Tudjman's goal was to oust the Serbs from the Krajina section of Croatia. His minions looted and burned Serb houses in order to force Krajina Serbs to flee Croatia for Banja Luka, Bosnia.

As a justification for the brutality of this forced migration, one high-level Croatian official, Vrhovnik, made the following retort to disapproving critics of the operation: "Recall the Old Testament saying: an eye for an eye, a tooth for a tooth."[12] That is, given the atrocities suffered by the Croats at the hands of the Serbs, the offensive action in Krajina was due justice.

Pleased by Croatia's advances toward an "ethnically pure state," Tudjman made public boasts. After the Croats ousted the Serbs, it was as if the Serbs had never lived there in the first place. Tudjman's vilification and expulsion of the Serbs from the Krajina gave him folk hero status among the ethnic Croats. By fueling the fires of interethnic conflict, Tudjman strengthened his own intraethnic power base.

These authoritarian elites have yet another tactic in their bag of tricks. In order to muster ethnic support for their own political ends, they manipulate the Western press. Leaders of the various republics have shown great ingenuity in their media tactics. The suffering of the Bosnian Muslims at the hands of the other factions has been well documented in the international press. That press rarely notes, however, the suffering of the Croats at the hands of the Muslims. The international media virtually ignores the suffering of the Serbs. The West seldom portrays the Serbs as victims; rather, it typecasts them as villains.

Ethnic leaders do not manipulate the press without the media's cooperation. Dramatic reports make good copy—"If it bleeds, it leads!" Hence, there is a tendency to create dichotomies of "good guys" versus "bad guys." Consider an example of bipolar reporting that exacerbates interethnic conflict. James Harff, director of an American public relations company employed by Bosnia and Croatia, made a statement in 1993 regarding ethnic conflict. When asked which achievement made him most proud, Harff replied that getting American Jews on the side of Bosnia and Croatia was his highest attainment:

> To have managed to put Jewish opinion on our side, . . . we could promptly equate the Serbs with the Nazis in the public mind. [He used words with high emotional content] . . . "ethnic cleansing," "concentration camp," which evoked images of Nazi Germany and the gas chamber of Auschwitz. The emotional charge was so powerful that nobody could go against it.[13]

Harff admitted that sometimes the information the company presented was not necessarily true. He defended himself by stating that, "Our work is not to verify information . . . Our work is to accelerate the circulation of information favorable to us . . . We are not paid to be moral."

Clearly, Croat and Muslim orchestration of the foreign media was an effective means of arousing international support against the Serbs. And by attaining support from abroad, they reinforced their domestic political stature. But the upside of gaining outside and intraethnic support had a downside of exacerbating interethnic tension.

Ethnic leaders also use cunning media tactics to rally their own people against other factions. One powerful mechanism employed by both the Croats and the Serbs in 1990–1991 was symbolic politics. They used the "transfiguration of the dead into martyrs" as a means to gather domestic support.

Both Tudjman and Milosevic trudged up secret histories to exhibit in the theater of symbolic politics. In particular, both camps launched campaigns to publicize massacres of Croats by Serb Cetniks, and of Serbs by the Croat Ustasa during the Civil War of 1941–1945. During that conflict the two main actors were the Serb Royalists, known as the Cetniks, and the Croat fascists, known as the Ustasa.

Each republic highlighted church ceremonies, excavations, and mass public reburials. Tudjman made an effort to create a new Croatian history that suppressed or minimized the negative experiences of the Croatian Serbs and publicized atrocities the Croats faced at the hands of the Cetniks. As a counterattack against Zagreb, Milosevic began his own propaganda campaign to ensure that the Croats would not forget that they had massacred Serbs. A series of stories recounting the Ustasa atrocities ran in Belgrade's main newspapers. In April 1991, there was a highly publicized documentary that recorded the entry into a cave in Bosnia-Herzegovina containing the remains of countless Serbs murdered by the Ustasa, Croat fascists from the Civil War. The discovery of bones throughout the region into the summer of 1991 reinforced the depiction of Croats as a "genocidal people."[14]

Each republic furthered their propaganda campaigns by placing major television and radio networks under strict government control. The full-force propaganda on both sides unleashed a "verbal civil war," which led to conflict escalation between Croats and Serbs. As citizens of each republic became glued to their television sets and radio receivers, each ethnic group, wherever they lived, mobilized against the other. They began taking a firm stance behind their ethnic leaders in the wake of this campaign of ethnonationalism. Hence, each authoritarian elite was successful in creating a common foe, securing a strong position of power, and exacerbating interethnic tensions.

In summary, two schools of thought explain why it is difficult to resolve ethnic conflicts: circumstance and choice. With respect to circumstance, this camp implies that conflicts are not only inevitable but also unmanageable. Ethnic conflicts derive from heterogeneous populations, and behavior stems from fear rather than gain. Hence, conflict prevention and resolution are difficult at best and foolhardy at worst. Ethnicity is destiny.

According to the choice school of thought, ethnicity is pretext. This camp implies that conflicts are not determined by circumstance but are the conscious decisions of political leaders. Thus, ethnic conflicts are manageable, and conflict prevention and resolution are possible. Conflicts stem from autocratic leaders whose behavior derives from gain. Hence, interventionists can deter and coerce and economic incentives might create collective action, cooperation, and political institutions.

Machiavellian manipulators do intensify ethnic differences. Yet, Bosnia and Kosovo are places where cultural and social institutions might be a source of conflict prevention and resolution. Social groups that cut across ethnic boundaries might lessen the negative political consequences of ethnic differences. Intermarriage among ethnic groups, coupled with regional economic approaches, is also a means of conflict resolution. Before interventionists can build such institutions for conflict resolution, however, they must understand the role ethnicity plays in conflicts among peoples. Ethnic differences per se are neither positive nor negative. Ethnicity becomes harmful only when leaders manipulate ethnic tensions for political gain.

CHAPTER SIX

OVERCOMING ETHNICITY

INSTITUTION BUILDING

UNDERSTANDING THE ROLE OF ETHNICITY in war-torn Bosnia and Kosovo is not the end of a process of institution building, it is the beginning. There is a need to rise above ethnicity, foster common cultural identity, and accept universal principles like human rights. This chapter discusses institution building, threat and promise, as well as collective goods and individual incentives in relation to the goal of rising above the constraints of ethnicity. In the context of successful coercion by outside powers, regional antagonists can engage in commerce and learn to cooperate. Post–Cold War Central European countries like Hungary, Poland, and the Czech Republic moved toward market economies without the need for coercive diplomacy by interventionist forces. In war-torn Bosnia and Kosovo, however, coercion and brute force were necessary before globalization could work its magic.

With respect to Bosnia, Dayton creates post-war governmental structures that include various ethnic groups but are not dominated by them. The agreement takes into account the fact that ethnic tensions exist primarily in the background of societal relations. Dayton seeks to avoid provoking long-standing internal animosities. Reconstruction proceeds to diffuse these tensions by involving most of the actors in conflict resolution. By engaging rather than isolating, Dayton also attempts to move minorities out of their basements of fear onto the streets of reconstruction.

The Dayton Accords attempt to foster a sense of common identity among erstwhile warring factions. Although it is not politically realistic, one approach is to facilitate political integration through the practice of elections and the establishment of parliamentary processes. Political factions might learn to build coalitions in order to achieve common goals. It is unlikely that integration of political institutions would precede the development of common social and economic bonds among factions. By encouraging groups to work together, interventionists seek to establish a critical mass for a common identity. In the aftermath of Dayton, distinctions like Serb or Croat remain but are not so intense that they result in violence.

In elite-dominated authoritarian situations, group-building methods, such as creating a federal system or granting local territorial autonomy to ethnic group leaders, might alleviate ethnic tensions. These approaches could subtly transform the existing balance of power thus creating a more stable situation. In addition, establishing a state bureaucracy staffed by multiple ethnicities might foster a sense of national unity.

Although integration through political interaction is a long shot in Bosnia and Kosovo, it is conceivable that a result of economic reconstruction might be political cooperation. Meanwhile, there is a tendency for ethnic in-group leaders to incite conflicts against out-groups for political gains. Once ethnic leaders cease assaulting other groups in order to establish political unity, there is a possibility for social cohesion to develop.

Social unity increases when majority populations respect the human rights of ethnic minorities. But to imagine that the Croats of Krajina would welcome back Serbs who once lived there is wishful thinking at best. And to envision that Serbs from Krajina would be gladly received in Kosovo is another example of overestimating the likelihood of desirable events.

When the basic rights of expression, existence, and safety are met, ethnic groups might be able to set aside their political differences. By establishing the integrity of basic human rights, interventionists seek to place ethnic tensions on the periphery of politics. But as long as politicians exploit interethnic conflict for intraethnic gain, human rights will not be viewed as a universal collective good. Meanwhile, policing the conflict arena takes precedence over political institution building.

At issue is whether ethnicity prevents the building of collective institutions. Those who assume that fighting in the Balkans is an inescapable consequence of historical ethnic differences also believe that it is not possible to build political institutions in this context.

But consider this comment about an American soldier stationed near Sarajevo, Staff Sergeant Paul Correale of Huber Heights, Ohio: "He has come to doubt the theory that the recent fighting in Bosnia was an inevitable continuation of longstanding ethnic antagonisms."[1] This statement suggests that the political leadership might be exploiting ethnicity in order to seize and hold power. With this knowledge in mind, foreign interventionists and local reconstructionists alike should take into account ethnic differences but also stress universal values like human rights.

Development of political institutions, creation of common social identity, and respect for human rights might also evolve from interethnic commerce. The transition from coercion to cooperation through commerce, however, is not a smooth route. As ethnic leaders throw obstacles in the path toward cooperation, the West must be prepared to use threat and promise to bring about collective action.

THREAT AND PROMISE

Threat and promise are two complementary approaches to procuring compliance. The threat camp assumes that individuals act on the basis of political greed and therefore need to be compelled. The promise camp presumes that they act on the basis of economic need and can be changed by rewards. Both threat and promise need to work hand and hand.

With respect to the concept of promise, consider the 1992 American presidential campaign statement, "It's the economy, stupid!"

This slogan was the mantra of Clintonites concerned with the domestic economic situation. The corresponding chant for interventionists and nation-builders who seek to rise above ethnicity is, "It's the global economy, stupid!" They promise to build a nation able to benefit from globalization on the foundation of commercial interaction.

Globalization of financial markets is the international counterpart to the focus on the domestic economy in the American presidential campaign. The assumption is that globalization would eventually trump tribalization in regions like the Balkans. Just as the magic of economic growth has lessened racial animosities in America, such wizardry might do wonders in Bosnia and Kosovo. Hence, the underlying logic of the Clinton policy in the Balkans is to move from coercion to cooperation through commerce. With respect to Bosnia, the promising geoeconomics of President Clinton in his second term is replacing the threatening geopolitics of President Bush and the Clinton first term. Although coercive diplomacy was still relevant at the close of the century, globalization and commercial diplomacy were making a headway.

Because outside powers pay greater attention to the links between force and diplomacy, the economic pillar frequently is the weakest link in the peace process. As opposed to spending for coercive diplomacy, applying funds toward economic diplomacy may speed the process of reconstruction. Consider the sums committed to military operations in contrast to sums committed to economic development. In Bosnia, military expenditures amount to about $5 billion per year, while about $1 billion per year goes for economic reconstruction.[2]

There is some progress in the transition of Bosnia to a market economy. Restoration of the economic infrastructure torn asunder in the fighting is slowly progressing. Because of some $2.1 billion of $5 billion in donor disbursed as of late 1998, there have been economic gains. Economic recovery has met initial projections, with growth of 50 percent in 1996, and 30 percent in 1997 and 1998. The very low starting base notwithstanding, such growth is a promising development. Although unemployment rates in Bosnia are at some 40 percent, unemployment has decreased precipitously from the post-war highs of 90 percent. Few other recent post-conflict cases, such as Cambodia and Guatemala, have recovered at such rapid rates as Bosnia.[3]

Over the long haul, commercial diplomacy should lessen the effect of ethnic differences in Bosnia and Kosovo. But ethnic differences will not simply dissolve as a result of presidential fiat and commercial engagement. Rather, coercion will still need to play a role in gaining the compliance of ethnic groups. In the context of a continued threat of military engagement against belligerents, the promise of commerce among the parties just might make some headway toward cooperation.[4]

COLLECTIVE GOODS
AND INDIVIDUAL INCENTIVES

The question remains how the pause in conflict afforded by Dayton allows for commerce to replace coercion. The answer to this question lies in continuing with a preponderance of outside power, while constructing a post-conflict environment amenable to a lasting peace. And the key to this solution is to create a balance of power through economic integration among the ethnic groups. The threat of military engagement was a means for coercive diplomacy; the promise of economic gain through commercial diplomacy might be a basis of cooperation. Because ethnic differences do not disappear as a result of commercial engagement, however, coercion is necessary to gain the compliance of ethnic groups in Bosnia.

A reason that commercial engagement might bring about political cooperation might be found in the theory of public goods. "Only a separate and 'individual' incentive will stimulate a rational individual in a latent group to act in a group-oriented way. In such circumstances group action can be obtained only through an incentive that operates, not indiscriminately, like the collective good, upon the group as a whole, but rather selectively toward the individuals in the group."[5] Bosnian Croats, Muslims, and Serbs must have selfish reasons to create a public good like overall security through political cooperation. Separate economic gains might be an individual incentive for each to cooperate for the sake of the collective good.

The Clinton administration approaches post-Dayton Bosnia as if it were a collective goods problem. Hence, the team downplays power and emphasizes economics over ethnicity. But the administration needs to retain a preponderance of external power while creating a balance of local power. Only in a context of preponderance or at least a balance of power can individual economic incentives facilitate collective action.

Outside interventionists need to work with moderate leaders on all sides to establish economic ties. Such links then might facilitate the growth of power sharing. The hope is that interethnic trade might persuade the elites that political interaction with their rivals is not a zero-sum game. That is, economic interaction may produce a "win-win-win" situation among the three basic groups in Bosnia. As a result of prospective economic gains, this approach envisions a scenario in which entrepreneurial activity forces the hand of corrupt political leaders.

Visions of future political harmony gained via present economic interaction had already become evident by October 1997. Without regard for ethnic identity, thieves deal in a Bosnian market of stolen cars from Western Europe. The thieves transport these automobiles and have a forum where onetime enemies bargain with one another for their individual incentives.[6] But only in the context of at least a minimum level of security against outside threat can such bargaining take place. It is in the overall interest of the "black marketers" to facilitate collective security in order to maintain their economic forum. When successful, such collective bargaining might be an incentive for further economic reconciliation.

The ethnic factions had engaged in commercial interactions even as early as 1996. Bosnian Croats, Muslims, and Serbs have been gathering at the "Arizona Market" in Brcko, Bosnia to sell black market commodities like brandy, cigarettes, blue jeans, and music cassettes. This market serves, "to remind outsiders that hatred, and even war, are rarely impediments to making money."[7] Obviously, stolen cars and black market goods cannot be a legitimate basis of economic integration and political development. The underlying principle, however, exemplifies the idea that integration ir-respective of ethnic identity is possible through economic coopera-tion and interdependence.

Surveys conducted from December 1996 through January 1997 indicate strong support for interethnic trade as route toward in-terethnic cooperation. Three USIA polls taken in Bosnia find that Bosnian Serbs favor interethnic trade with the Bosnian Croats by a margin of 55 percent, and with the Bosnian Muslims by a margin of 47 percent. The Bosnian Croats and Muslims are even more opti-mistic. Some 67 percent of the Bosnian Croats polled favored trade with the Serbs and 61 percent favored trade with the Muslims. The Bosnian Muslims reported economic cooperation with the Serbs and Croats at 76 percent and 86 percent, respectively. One member of a focus group in Banja Luka felt that, "economic relations with the Muslims . . . are inevitable. Money and business do not recognize any borders. Neither ethnic, nor ethical ones."[8]

Another example of successful ethnic interaction can be seen at a gas station in Kiseljak, Bosnia. "When Dragan Kozovic pulls up be-hind Esad Hamzic at the gas station and Ivan Barisic fills their tanks, it is the Bosnian peace accord at work. Kozovic is a Serb. Hamzic is a Muslim. Barisic is a Croat." The gas station owner exclaimed:

> Take a look at these two guys. They both look the same. They both dress the same. They both eat the same. They even drive sim-ilar cars. The only reason they were killing each other are their names and their religions. . . . What a bloody, deadly and stupid absurdity. . . . If there is a way that all this horror will be forgot-ten, it will be because of things like this gas station. Money talks.[9]

Given the tensions among the ethnic groups, it is a surprise that support for interethnic commercial activity is so high. It should be a task of the Western interventionists to help foster this desire for eco-nomic cooperation. But only in the context of preponderant or bal-anced power can the West hope that individual economic incentives can facilitate collective political action.

In an interview, a Croatian diplomat acknowledged the role of the United States in providing economic incentives for political cooperation among the ethnic groups. When asked, "What were the carrots and sticks offered by the United States to bring about the [Bosnian-Croat] Federation?" He replied, "Basically the carrots were stopping the conflict, starting economic development, and over time regulating the relations with Croatia itself and with the rest of Europe."[10] Not only did the answer omit any reference to "sticks," negative incentives for building the federation, the interviewee also focused exclusively on economic rewards, or "carrots." An assumption underlying his answer was that the Western military presence would be a constant feature of the Bosnian landscape. Consider the effect of outside military forces.

In the presence of NATO military power, economic collaboration might be a means by which Croats, Muslims, and Serbs downplay their ethnic differences and build Bosnian institutions for conflict resolution. In addition to maintaining a military presence, the international community should provide economic development funds and civil assistance to the parties. Indeed, in Annex 10 of the Dayton Peace Agreement on Civilian Implementation, the parties call for the appointment of an international coordinator to facilitate civilian aspects of the peace settlement. These include "humanitarian aid, economic reconstruction, protection of human rights, and the holding of free elections."[11]

Civil affairs units of NATO provide necessities like sanitation, food, and water, which should facilitate the growth of a stable environment for commercial transactions among the ethnic groups. In preparation for deployment to Banja Luka, Bosnia, an American army reservist discussed the provision of basic necessities that underlay economic incentives. She said, "Our Civil Affairs unit serves as a liaison between the government and the population. We go in post-conflict and provide sanitation, food, and water."[12]

But who receives the benefits of civil assistance and economic development aid? One critic of the Clinton administration's approach in Bosnia claims that 98 percent of the American economic assistance has gone to the Bosnian-Croat Federation, and only two percent to Republika Srpska.[13]

While American assistance may be distributed unequally among the parties, the official U.S. Army policy is to assist all three ethnic factions. Nevertheless, many American soldiers sympathize with the Muslims. The troops believe that the Muslims have suffered the most during the Bosnian War. In contrast with the official policy of treating the three ethnic groups equally, Washington in fact denies aid to the Bosnian Serbs because of "noncompliance with Dayton." While it makes sense to refrain from providing economic assistance to those who fail to comply, it makes little sense to require that local officials from Srpska meet standards not required of those from the federation. Mayors in the Bosnian Serb Republic had to make written certification of their support of multiethnicity in order to qualify for U.S. aid. That requirement was not applied in Muslim and Croat regions, thus exacerbating ethnic tensions.[14]

One should not expect leaders of the Republika Srpska to build common political institutions unless they share some of the economic benefits. Indeed, as Sarajevo as well as other cities around the federation experience an economic boom, Republika Srpska has high unemployment. And because these leaders receive inequitable treatment in the presence of Western military power, they may have even less incentive to cooperate if the outside military presence were withdrawn.

This chapter discussed institution building, threat and promise, as well as collective goods and individual incentives. At issue are conditions under which antagonists can rise above ethnicity. In the event of coercive diplomacy by interventionists, local parties can become involved in commerce and learn to build political institutions. Given this sunny long-term scenario, the next chapter considers immediate scenarios and policy options for Bosnia and Kosovo.

CHAPTER SEVEN

SCENARIOS AND POLICIES FOR BOSNIA AND KOSOVO

IN LIGHT OF THE DISCUSSION of cultural and economic approaches to conflict resolution, consider the significance of Bosnia and Kosovo. The two scripts for both cases are war, on one hand, versus no war, no peace, on the other hand. Outcomes for Bosnia include partition, a single state, and de facto partition. To anticipate the conclusions below, de facto or informal partition—one in which groups live in geographically isolated areas but without formal partition—is the most viable outcome for Bosnia, complemented by arms control and economic integration.

The term "partition" has a different significance in the cases of Bosnia and Kosovo. For Bosnia, legal or formal partition means separation of a multiethnic state into at least two parts. The Muslim leadership in Sarajevo adamantly opposes division of the state which, in February 1999 included Bosnian Muslims, Western Christians (Roman Catholic Croats), and Eastern Orthodox Christians (Bosnian Serbs). Partition would separate the Bosnian Federation of Muslims and Catholic Croats from Republika Srpska with its Orthodox Christians.

For Kosovo, formal partition has two meanings: creating an independent state for all of Kosovo by taking the province out of Serbia or dividing Kosovo itself into parts. With respect to an independent state, partition would divide a province that was 90 percent ethnic-Albanian Muslim from Orthodox Christian Yugoslavia. The Muslim leadership in Pristina strongly favors partition of Kosovo from Serbia. Just as resolutely, Belgrade opposes partition and even autonomy. At issue is whether there is a solution that would satisfy the ethnic-Albanian desire for independence as well as Belgrade's requirement of maintaining the territorial integrity of Serbia by retaining one of its medieval homelands. Although informal partition may not satisfy either side, it might be the only compromise that even begins to resolve the conflict over Kosovo.

History versus Demography

With respect to the traditional importance of Kosovo for Serbia, consider the musings of an ardent Serbian nationalist. When asked what sacrifices a Serb would make to retain his ancient homeland that is full of medieval icons, he pondered, then said that he would "do anything to keep Kosovo, except, of course, to live there or die for it!" In other words, Serbs speak and write as if Kosovo were of great importance to them, but are unwilling to make a home in that province. Serbian reluctance to reside in Kosovo suggests that migration and demography eventually might have created a situation where that province was 100 percent ethnic Albanian. In order to forestall such a possibility, Belgrade drove over a million ethnic Albanians from Kosovo during spring 1999.

Consider the demographic situation before the 1999 hostilities in Kosovo. Only about one person out of ten was Serb, and ethnic-Albanian mothers gave birth to 15 babies for every Serb child. If Belgrade had not driven ethnic Albanians from Kosovo within the next two decades, Serbs might have been a minority not just in Kosovo but also within the whole of Serbia.

In addition to the demographic transition that favored the ethnic-Albanian population, Serbs were steadily emigrating from Kosovo. During the 1960s, about a quarter of a million Serbs lived in that province, while there were only about 180,000 Serbs in Kosovo almost four decades later.[1] Belgrade feared that any form of autonomy for the Kosovars might have accelerated the outflow of Serbs from their ancient homeland, encourage immigration of other ethnic Albanians from neighboring countries to Kosovo, and further destabilize the area.

Strategic Significance

As in the profession of real estate, the field of strategic studies emphasizes "location, location, location." The strategic import of Bosnia and Kosovo stem from perceptions of geography and history. If conflict in either unit were to escalate and expand, it might do so along confessional (religious) fault lines. States with large Muslim populations like Bosnia, Albania, and Turkey might line up against the Orthodox Christian states of Serbia, Greece, and even Russia.[2] Because confessional conflicts have a long history in the Balkans, it is not unreasonable to envision religious-based conflicts again in that region.

Bosnia. The predecessors of the Bosnian Muslims were the Ottoman invaders of Europe. They viewed Bosnia as an opening to both Orthodox and Catholic Christendom. The Ottoman Turks envisioned Bosnia as a dagger pointing westward toward Catholic Christianity. Indeed, around the year 1500, Bosnia constituted part of the eastern boundary of Western civilization. Orthodox Christianity and Islam were east of Bosnia; Western Christianity was west of Bosnia.[3]

In addition, Bosnia was a gateway in the creation of a Greater Serbia. Bosnia was an intermediate region linking Serbs in Belgrade to those in the Krajina region of Croatia. Indeed, advocates of a Greater Croatia perceived Croats in Bosnia as wards of Zagreb. But dreams of Greater Serbia and Greater Croatia were nightmares for the Muslims of Bosnia. Fortunately for them, Serb and Croat fantasies floundered on the shoals of the Dayton peace process.

Kosovo. Like Bosnia, the strategic consequence of Kosovo also derives from its geopolitical position. Control of Kosovo provides access to Albania. Indeed, imagery of a Greater Albania includes eventual unity among ethnic Albanians wherever they are located. If war were to erupt between Serbia and the ethnic Albanians of Kosovo, Tirana declared that it would be forced "to act as one nation." The sporadic hostilities in Kosovo run a higher risk of internationalization than conflict in nearby Bosnia.

Combat in Kosovo reverberates in Albania, Bulgaria, Greece, and Turkey. Likewise, instability in Albania might expand to the ethnic–Albanian minority in the former Yugoslav Republic of Macedonia. Ethnic Albanians in Kosovo might establish close ties with their brethren in Macedonia, Turkey, and Bulgaria. Indeed, the history of Macedonia reflects conflicts between Greek orthodoxy and Muslims of the Ottoman Empire.

Because Ankara would have strengthened its strategic position with additional allies in Kosovo, Albania, and Macedonia, Athens might take notice. The perceived threat to Greece's northern frontier would be greater in the context of instabilities spreading from Kosovo. And even though Greece is a member of the Western alliance, deterioration of Balkan security might induce Athens to strengthen its links with the tacit Orthodox coalition that is on the rise.

New Fault Lines of Europe

During the Cold War, the single fault line in Europe was between East and West—between dictatorial communism and democratic capitalism. In the post–Cold War era, two new lines divide the continent: North-South and East-West. The first line divides the wealthy North from the impoverished South; the second line separates Christendom into Eastern Orthodox and Western Christianity, including Catholics and Protestants. Located in southeastern Europe, the Balkans lie on the religious fault line, a precipitous situation further exacerbated by the presence of Muslim vestiges from the Ottoman Empire.

In the aftermath of NATO expansion, the alliance includes former Warsaw Pact countries—the Czech Republic, Hungary, and Poland—as member states. Consequently, NATO enlargement creates a new fault line in Europe. There is an upscale Europe of NATO members concerned with global issues of monetary union, trade flows, and worldwide financial investment. Because of their economic wealth and military power, they contrast sharply with countries in poor areas of Europe. Its populations remain haunted by historical tribalism, ancient hatreds, and memories of ethnic battles.

Western Christians—Catholics and Protestants—populate rich regions of Europe. Eastern Orthodox Christians inhabit poor Europe. NATO is like a wealthy country club that excludes neighbors who live near the club, but who are socially not acceptable as members. And the excluded poor cannot understand why the rich members of NATO seek to protect non Christians in Bosnia and Kosovo, entities with Muslim populations left over from Ottoman efforts to conquer Europe.

In writing about Kosovo and the new fault line of Europe, one commentator worries that a pro-Greek, pro-Serb and anti-Turkish Russia stocked with loose nuclear weapons might be drawn into a conflict that arises out of the instability in Kosovo. Even a "Theater war that fuses Balkan and Middle Eastern hatreds is not out of the question."[4]

SCENARIO I FOR BOSNIA: WAR

Dance of the Diplomats

Although Bosnia and Kosovo are two sides of the same coin of political instability in the Balkans, the Dayton Accords addressed Bosnia but ignored Kosovo. The diplomats at Dayton reinforced a ceasefire in Bosnia, while they danced around the conflict in Kosovo. Not surprisingly, an armed insurgency in Kosovo escalated after Dayton. The ethnic–Albanian leadership in Pristina was amazed that Dayton never addressed the fate of Kosovo.

While the Bosnian Croats, Muslims, and Serbs danced with the diplomats at Dayton, ethnic Albanians in Kosovo were the wallflowers of the Balkans. The lesson learned was that revolt got the attention of the Great Powers. The West paid attention only to those groups in the former Yugoslavia that rebelled. Hence, the Kosovars had to revolt against Serbia in order to gain independence, or at least to reacquire autonomy. With respect to Kosovo, Dayton was a point of departure for a recurrence of war in the Balkans.

Resumption of Hostilities

The war scenario for Bosnia assumes that the Croats, Muslims, and Serbs of Bosnia will continue to bicker and are unable or unwilling to make a lasting peace among them, that the de facto partition of Bosnia will become formalized, and that sporadic fighting will resume because NATO is unwilling to enforce the ceasefire. In this scenario, a fear of Western casualties drives decisionmaking in Bonn, London, Paris, and Washington.

Further, despite the president's decision in December 1997 to retain 12,000 American troops in Bosnia, assume that the Congress passes a joint resolution in the year 2000 calling for the withdrawal of those troops by the year 2001. The other members of the original 30-plus nation coalition will also state intentions to withdraw, and peacekeeping missions will flounder.

The resumption of fighting in Bosnia would begin to overlap combat in Kosovo. A resumption of hostilities would deepen ethnic divisions and exacerbate the refugee situation. In addition, the quasi states involved in the Bosnian fighting would find themselves hard-pressed to support both the increased number of refugees and their own military forces. This shortage of resources would foster plans for conquest of neighboring territories, if only to secure new munitions and foodstuffs.

The intensity of the level of combat would increase as politicians engaged in outbidding, thereby exaggerating ethnic divisions. Consequently, there would be a ripple effect in the region. For every slight against Serbs in Krajina, Srpskan forces would retaliate. For every insult against Serbs in Kosovo, Belgrade would authorize reprisal raids against Kosovars.

As the practice of ethnic outbidding became commonplace, allies in neighboring states, such as Croatia and Serbia, would reenter the fighting over Bosnia. But this bleak future need not be an inevitable consequence of "ancient hatreds." There is an historical precedent for interventionist forces to maintain the ceasefire in the Balkans. During May and June 1997, the United Nations Preventive Deployment Force (UNPREDEP) had been active in preventing the further escalation and expansion of conflict along the border between the Former Yugoslav Republic of Macedonia (FYROM) and Albania.

But consider a phased reduction of the military component of UNPREDEP. During the spring of 1999, fighting in Kosovo increased between ethnic Albanians and Serbs, and this combat spread to Macedonia. If ethnic Albanians in Macedonia and Montenegro join the fighting, it would provide an incentive for other countries to enter the hostilities.

As a result of combat in Macedonia, there might be casualties among American soldiers deployed there under the United Nations flag. As the twentieth century closes, politicians opposed to the use of U.S. forces in peacekeeping operations would make fiery speeches on Capitol Hill demanding the withdrawal of Americans from both Macedonia and Bosnia.[5]

Ethnic Albanians in the Kosovo region of Serbia have stepped up their activities in favor of independence. Radical Kosovars engaged in sabotage against Serbian installations and launched terror attacks against Serbian nationals in Kosovo. Belgrade cracked down on the Kosovars. The hundreds of thousands of ethnic-Albanian refugees demanded help from Albania, a country that has a 70 percent Muslim population.

To return to the scenario concerning the impact of a resumption of fighting in Bosnia, Tirana might move toward countries with large Muslim populations at odds with the United States. In return, Albania would receive arms and volunteers from Muslim nations. Foot soldiers would arrive from Iran, Afghanistan, and the Sudan. Future collaboration between Albania and Islamist groups would present the United States with a dilemma. On one hand, Washington would like to strengthen Albania against Serbia; on the other hand, the United States would like to avoid allowing radicals to use Albania as a platform for spreading terrorism throughout Europe.

During August 1998, there was an effort to bomb the U.S. Embassy in Tirana. American officials implicated a close associate of Osama bin Laden in the terrorist bombing plot. Bin Laden is an "Islamist," a radical follower of Islam, who calls for the murder of American soldiers and civilians. Washington pressured Tirana to extradite the suspect to Cairo. In retaliation for the extradition of his operatives, bin Laden may have encouraged the bombing of American embassies in Kenya and Tanzania.[6]

Also during 1998, Tirana launched a full-scale crackdown on Islamist groups. Because of impoverished and chaotic situation, these groups had been using Albania as a haven from Western law enforcement agencies. Additionally, the Islamists had built a terrorist infrastructure. In this respect, Albania has the potential of becoming a platform for worldwide terrorist operations.

Albania received technical assistance from Western intelligence agencies. With this aid, Tirana expelled two Egyptian groups—Islamic Jihad and al-Gama'at al-Islamiyya (the Islamic Group).[7] Islamic Jihad is an Egyptian group accused of working with the Saudi businessman turned terrorist financier, Osama bin Laden. Active since the late 1970s, the Islamic Group is an indigenous Egyptian extremist group dedicated to the overthrow of the secular government of Egypt and its replacement with an Islamic regime. Egyptian authorities blame Islamic Jihad for the attempted assassination of the Prime Minister of Egypt in 1993. These authorities also accuse al-Gama'at of killing 58 tourists in Luxor Egypt in November 1997.

Along with the Islamic Salvation Army of Algeria, assume that the two Egyptian groups begin to reacquire a foothold in Albania. In light of the outbreak of fighting along the borders between Albania and Kosovo, Tirana would have to choose between obtaining the support of Islamists or being further destabilized. Presume that Albania chooses to use the Islamists at the risk of being taken over by them. Tirana would then trade off the benefit of collaborating with Washington for the assistance that Islamists might provide against Serbia.

Although Albania is wary of Islamist revolutionaries, the expectation of an alignment among states with large Muslim populations derives from the war in Bosnia between 1992 and 1995. During this war, the Islamic Republic of Iran supported the Bosnian Muslim regime against Christian Orthodox Serbia and the Bosnian Serbs.[8]

Although it is unlikely, there is an historical precedent for a predominantly Muslim nation like Albania to align itself with radical Islam in order to protect itself against Serbia. Sarajevo also used bin

Laden in its war against Bosnian Serbs and Serbia. Recall from chapter 2 that Washington gave a green light for Zagreb to receive arms from Tehran en route to Sarajevo. But this traffic signaling resulted in a policy debacle. Consequently, it is improbable that the United States would give another hint that it approved of Islamist arms and volunteers helping a Muslim state in Europe—Albania.

But in order to block Islamist intervention on behalf of Albania, the United States would need to take forceful action. In view of the reluctance of Washington to stop the fighting, Belgrade could send regular army units, ostensibly to help the minority Serb population in Kosovo, but in fact they could eliminate entirely the militant ethnic Albanians. Meanwhile, expansion of combat across Bosnia's borders would result in the shipment of heavy weapons by Serbia to its Bosnian Serb allies. Neighboring countries would draw on stocks of armaments unaffected by the Dayton Accords and Stabilization Force (SFOR) limitations.

Zagreb would send regular units from Croatia to assist the Bosnian Croats. Tehran would reestablish its arms pipeline to Sarajevo in cooperation with Zagreb but also independent of Croatia. With the introduction of military units from Belgrade, Srpskan forces might use their combined preponderance of military force to resume their practice of ethnic cleansing of Bosnian Muslims.

If fighting resumes, there is little possibility for transitioning from coercion to commerce. The provision of selective incentives to stimulate collective political action would become the first casualty of the war scenario. Although the likelihood of the war scenario for Bosnia is slim, the spring 1999 fighting in Kosovo increases the likelihood of a resumption of hostilities in Bosnia.

SCENARIO II FOR BOSNIA:
NO WAR, NO PEACE

The second scenario foresees neither war nor peace coming to Bosnia. As a result of partial implementation of the Dayton Peace Agreement, the status quo holds and there is some payoff from the provision of selective incentives. There would be growth in political

institutions across the Bosnian Federation and the Republika Srpska. Although Croatia and Serbia would not formally agree to respect the sovereign equality of one another and to settle their
disputes by peaceful means, both states would act as if they were not
at war. The NATO-established ceasefire would remain in effect, but
the parties would continue to argue about the future.

This bickering would slow down efforts by the Bosnian Federation to reap the benefits of a lack of warfare. An attempt to join the
European Union would be a nonstarter. The goal of membership
would be to use the promise of the marketplace to overcome ethnic
rivalry. Although the West would like to emphasize geoeconomics
over realpolitik, the regional actors would prefer politics to economics. Hence, Bosnia would fail to become a part of the global
economy. But the partial economic success of Bosnia would help
break down some of the barriers of ethnicity. In the context of a
move toward globalization, ethnicity would not be destiny. Although "no war, no peace" is a sunny scenario, it has more chance
to see the light of day than the bleak war scenario.

The second scenario anticipates that the parties are willing to
develop economic ties among themselves, but that the pace of implementation of Dayton lags behind economic integration. Formal
partition becomes unthinkable with ongoing economic collaboration. NATO's military presence would continue to maintain the
ceasefire, and Congress would support the American deployment to
Bosnia in the absence of casualties.

Low-level hostility would continue as the Bosnian Federation
and the Republika Srpska jockey for position in the region. With the
presence of Western military forces and growing economic ties,
there would be a de facto partition—political autonomy without
legal separation. Given this political reality of no war, no peace, the
lure of the global and regional marketplace may be one way to
avoid a resumption of the fighting and transcend ethnic animosities.
In the context of the ceasefire, there is a growing likelihood of a
transition from coercion to commerce. Selective incentives would
begin to stimulate collective political action.

The magic of the marketplace is an incentive for individuals to
escape from politicians who would use ethnicity in their bid for

power. The Arizona market in Brcko would become a model for other locations in Bosnia like Tuzla. Bosnian Croats, Muslims, and Serbs would cut deals on such commodities as brandy, books, and blue jeans. Economic collaboration would begin to foster common cultural identity, and universal principles like human rights would become accepted as part of the rules of the game of interethnic trade.

The no war, no peace scenario for Bosnia is simply an extension of a pattern from the status quo of the late 1990s. The scenario for Bosnia is much brighter than the script for Kosovo.

OUTCOMES FOR BOSNIA

In view of this discussion of war and no war, no peace for Bosnia, the question arises as to what outcomes follow these two scenarios.

The three outcomes for Bosnia are formal partition of Bosnia into separate entities for Bosnian Croats, Muslims, and Serbs; a multiethnic federated state; and de facto partition of Bosnia along with arms control and economic integration of autonomous entities. To anticipate the most likely conclusion for Bosnia, economic integration may lead to political cooperation under the protection of external military power. Now consider three policy alternatives in order.

The controversy involves policy outcomes and the differences in attitudes among ethnic groups. Politicians who preach ancient hatreds would have outsiders believe that ethnicity is destiny. But ethnicity may not be a barrier to economic integration. Political unity, however, is less likely in view of these popular, divisive attitudes. There is a fault line between those who favor partitioning into multiple entities and those who support a single multiethnic state. In connection with Bosnia, some believe that the three ethnic groups can live peacefully in the country. In contrast, others say that, "There is no living together anymore. As the saying goes, once a loaf of bread is broken in two, there's no more putting it together."

A USIA poll conducted in January of 1997 found that 79 percent of Bosnian Serbs and 82 percent of Bosnian Croats felt that the war has done too much damage for peaceful coexistence. Only Bosnian Muslims were optimistic about the likelihood of peace, by a margin of 84 percent. A USIA poll conducted in June of 1996, is illustrative of the Bosnian Serb and Croat pessimism toward peaceful coexistence. The study reports that 96 percent of the Bosnian Serbs and 90 percent of the Croats found partition to be inevitable, while eight in ten Bosnian Muslims disagree with that finding.[9]

Outcome I: Partition along Ethnic Lines? No!

Underlying the policy for partition is whether the peace process in the Balkans pays sufficient attention to ethnic differences. At issue is the extent to which Dayton's goal of maintaining the territorial integrity of Bosnia should give way to some form of partition.[10] The basic reason that partition is a nonstarter is because it is unlikely to produce stability in the long run. Even though de facto partition along ethnic lines is a political reality, partition without economic integration in Bosnia is unlikely to produce long-term political stability.[11]

There is little doubt that politicians who exploit ethnic differences dominate the political landscape of the Balkans. There are two reasons why these political leaders are successful. They have considerable popularity, and attitudes divide along ethnic lines.

Two schools of thought address the idea of single or multiple states for the area that is Bosnia. The first school presumes that partitioning Bosnia would allow for a balance among its ethnic groups. Such a balance would lead to a peaceful resolution of disputes and security for all. A second assumes that partition would create a preponderance of power in favor of Serbia and result in the domination of the Muslim population by the Bosnian Serbs.

In addition, the second school of thought asserts that partition would reward aggression, validate ethnic cleansing, and allow war criminals to remain at large. In the context of arms control among the parties, there is a possibility that de facto partition might balance the power without reigniting the fighting. But the downside of partition far outweighs any perceived benefits. These costs consist of refugee creation, social disintegration, ethnic politics, and conflict expansion.

Refugee Creation and Economic Decline

While partition has been advanced many times during the twentieth century as a solution to conflict, there are major problems with partition as a policy option. Refugee creation is an inevitable consequence of partition. Upheaval occurs as ethnic groups try to readjust geographically to new boundaries.

Following the partition of India in 1947, some 17.2 million people crossed from India into the Islamic Republic of Pakistan and vice versa. Incidents of violence between Muslim and Hindu refugee groups were commonplace, with whole refugee trains attacking one another when they met on the road.[12] Large-scale migration occurs as refugees and postpartition minority groups relocate to homogenous territories.

In connection with the former Yugoslavia, there are reports that more than one million Bosnians remained displaced within the borders of the republic by the time the Dayton Peace Agreement was signed in December 1995. Complicating the issue, a USIA poll conducted in June of 1996 finds strong sentiment among refugees of each ethnic group that they cannot move freely throughout the country (81 percent of Bosnian Serbs, 87 percent of Bosnian Croats, and 87 percent of Bosnian Muslims).[13]

In addition to the refugees remaining in Bosnia, at least one million more were refugees in some 25 other European countries. They resided primarily in the neighboring republics of the former Yugoslavia and throughout Western Europe.[14] The four years of conflict in the region created an estimated 2.7 million refugees. This figure represents approximately 14 percent of the combined population of Bosnia, Croatia, and Serbia, some 18.3 million people.[15] Formal partition would only add to the number of refugees created by war.

As a result of such widespread emigration, newly created entities, such as the Bosnia envisioned under the Dayton Accords, find themselves overwhelmed with the problems of populations on the move. Public resources can be drained by such tasks as setting up and running refugee camps, policing orderly movement within the country, preventing the outbreak of further violence among different ethnic groups, and the eventual relocation and resettlement of the refugees. The movement of both capital and labor diminishes economic productivity, which may take years to reach prepartition levels of performance. The war in Bosnia has already produced a decline in the economic output of the warring parties.

The war has caused production to plummet, unemployment and inflation to soar, and has exacerbated human misery. No economic statistics for 1992–1995 are available, although output clearly has fallen substantially below the levels of earlier years and almost certainly is well below one thousand dollars per head.

The prewar level of per capita income in the former Yugoslavia was $1,980. In 1995, it dropped 70 percent and stood at $600. By the end of the war in 1995, GDP had shrunk by 70 percent to about $2.5 billion. The postwar primary economic engine is the trade and commerce resulting from the reconstruction effort itself. Industrial production during the first nine months of 1996 increased by 60 percent in comparison to the previous year, but was still only 9 percent of the prewar level.[16]

Social Disintegration

In addition to the economic consequences, there is the issue of the deterioration of social links both within and among ethnic groups. Because partition cannot hope to relocate ethnic groups in completely homogenous units, there will be geographical areas that remain ethnically heterogeneous.

Contact between family and friends left behind does not stop with partition. Ties between members of ethnic groups who leave and those who stay behind remain strong. Constant communication occurs on an intraethnic group level, despite geographic demarcation and distance. For example, Krajina Serbs expelled from Croatia retain their ties to their kin in the region, rather than building loyalty to Croatia. There are bound to be tensions within Croatia, given the presence of Serbs who remain in the region but are loyal to Serbia not Croatia.

How Zagreb treats its Serbs is the mirror in which Serbs elsewhere view Croatia. Thus, majority treatment of minorities is a source for further conflict. Once partition establishes ethnically homogenous entities, maltreatment of minorities within units of differing ethnicity becomes a legitimate source of friction. Ethnic majorities seek to redress wrongs done to their kin in neighboring areas, which can lead to armed conflict. Should the Bosnian Federation deny local Serbs civil rights, Republika Srpska may act to redress those wrongs—even though Serbs in the Bosnian Federation are not Srpskan citizens.

Ethnic Politics

Another difficulty with partition is its effect on ethnic politics. When partition occurs along ethnic boundaries, it creates classes of disenfranchised citizens; ethnic minorities become majorities and vice versa.[17] Consider the process of partitioning Ireland in the early 1920s. When the British elected to split Ireland into the Catholic south and Protestant north, that decision created minorities in both states. Southern Protestants and northern Catholics suddenly found themselves bereft of the status they enjoyed under unified British rule. Tens of thousands crossed the border in an effort to remain part of a majority group. Partition, based on ethnicity, creates new entities. Minorities, however, invariably remain among the majority population.

Citizenship in these new quasi states derives from ethnic or religious identity. Partition along ethnic lines infuses the new entities with the right to rule. This right is without regard for those designated as the "other."[18] As a result, minority groups suffer. Unable or unwilling to leave what they believe to be their homeland, these people become second-class citizens under the new government.

Denied fundamental rights to property, political participation, economic prosperity, and religious freedom, minorities can quickly become a source of further conflict. Because they cannot participate as full citizens, minority groups may turn to violence to achieve their goals. This in turn can lead to further partitioning, as minorities choose the path of secession rather than participation.

Bosnian Serbs claim to be denied equal status in the Bosnian Federation. This claim gave them a pretext for creating Republika Srpska, which is hesitant to become incorporated into the multiethnic federation specified in the Dayton Peace Agreement. But the international community does not assign either Pale or Banja Luka the same status as Belgrade, Sarajevo, and Zagreb. In order to bolster its diplomatic position in the postwar period, leaders in Srpska imply that the ceasefire might not hold. A new war would result in both escalation and expansion beyond that of the pre-Dayton conflict.

Expansion across Borders

A further problem with partition is in its effect on the expansion of conflict. Partition can externalize internal conflicts. When the factors of repressed minority groups and habitual external intervention combine, the line blurs between civil conflict and interstate conflict.[19] Ethnic minority groups are quick to look for outside aid, especially across their own borders. Minorities enlist the aid of newly partitioned states of like ethnic origin. Thus, Radovan Karadzic's Srpskan allies pressure Belgrade for support, despite international calls for his arrest and prosecution for war crimes.

Similarly, minority groups appeal for help to those interventionist nations that favor partition. Nations become aligned with opposing sides, and conflict expands beyond local boundaries. Formal partition increases the likelihood that external supporters enter an internal conflict and make it an international war. Prior to the outbreak of hostilities in the spring of 1999, the international community had contained the fighting in the former Yugoslavia within the confines of the republics. But the greater the number of independent entities in that area, the higher the likelihood that internal disputes become external conflicts.

Given the negative consequences of the partition policy outcome, it fits most appropriately with the war scenario. Fortunately, however, there is a low likelihood of both war and partition in the Balkans.

Outcome II: Single Multiethnic Federal State? No!

Just as the war scenario is improbable, a peace scenario based upon a single multiethnic federal state is also unlikely. Though implausible, it is necessary to explicate this policy option associated with the peace scenario. Such a single state would have to overcome ethnic tensions, resettle refugees, maintain the ceasefire, prosecute war criminals, establish a federal constitution, hold national elections, and work to rebuild the nation as a whole.

A multiethnic Bosnian state is neither politically feasible nor would it be stable in the long run.[20] Just as a sunny peace scenario may not see the light of day, nor might the single state policy option. But a third policy may be feasible. It builds upon the informal patterns of separation, order of battle, and commercial transactions.

Outcome III: De Facto Partition, Arms Control, and Economic Integration? Yes!

The third and preferred policy outcome is to reinforce informal political autonomy. In the section on Outcome I, there is a discussion of formal partition. Outcome III derives from the informal, de facto separation on the ground. In addition, the nonlegal partition of Outcome III requires a build up of the weaker Bosnian Muslims and a build down of the stronger Serbian side.

With respect to weapons, Annex 1B of the Dayton Peace Agreement contains provisions for arms control. The parties agreed to establish regional arms control arrangements. They also agreed to refrain from the importation of any heavy weapons into the region for a period of 90 days while arms control negotiations took place. And they agreed not to import heavy armaments for a period of 180 days from the signature of the agreement if the talks failed to establish an arms control accord. Because of the failure to reach an agreement on arms control, these provisions of Dayton need to be revisited.

In the presence of a preponderance of external power, the goal would be to effect a local balance of power among the parties. Arms supplies to the Muslims and Croats of the Bosnian Federation might balance Srpskan military strength. As previously noted, Bosnian Serb military capabilities stem from Belgrade's retention of prewar stocks of the former Yugoslavia.

In compliance with the Dayton Peace agreement and as of August 1997, the Bosnian Serbs destroyed 68 tanks, 9 armored combat vehicles, and 202 artillery pieces in the Republika Srpska. Meanwhile, in the Federation of Bosnia and Herzegovina, the Muslims destroyed 535 artillery pieces. These totals represent about 30 percent of the Dayton Peace agreement's requirements.[21] In order to bring about a local balance, build up should occur even if there is no build down of Bosnian Serb weapons.

In fiscal year 1996 alone, Congress authorized the transfer of $100 million in defense articles and services to train and equip Bosnian Federated Forces: 46,100 rifles, 1,000 machine guns, 6,592 radios and tactical telephones, 45 tanks, 80 armored personnel carriers, 840 light antitank weapons, and 15 utility helicopters. All items were to be mission-capable and supported by necessary maintenance equipment and replacement parts.[22]

In addition to arms control, economic collaboration is a prerequisite for the success of autonomy. Without economic integration, de facto partition is a formula for tragedy. Should the political status quo hold, it is imperative to work toward economic coordination between the Bosnian Federation and the Republika Srpska, as well as among Bosnia, Croatia, and Serbia.

There also needs to be cooperation among the parties on common projects. In this regard, Secretary of State Madeleine Albright said, "If these kinds of communal projects do not go forward, the kinds of projects that help to knit the multiethnic society together, then there will not be American assistance."[23] Secretary Albright suggests using American leverage in order to encourage social and economic integration. In this respect, the State Department has launched a Southeast European Action Plan. The goals are to assist in the consolidation of reform within individual states, encourage cooperation within the region, and advance the region's integration into Europe as a whole.

Despite its polyglot distribution of ethnicities, Bosnia's economic infrastructure remains distributed throughout the country as a whole.[24] For either the Republika Srpska or the Bosnian Federation to become truly prosperous each requires the economic interaction of the other. It is not enough to establish economic links with the outside; achieving full growth demands a reestablishment of the national economy. Given increased trade among equals, Croats,

Muslims, and Serbs can work to reconstruct a common identity as Bosnians. But economic integration is unlikely if any one group has political control over another.

In principle, Bosnia-Herzegovina remains a single economic unit, but de facto political partition prevents that economic unit from functioning effectively. The de facto partition that exists even under the Dayton Accords limits the productivity of the nation as a whole. Encouraging increased food production and exchange between Srpskan grain farmers in the north and Muslim food processing plants in the south might help to raise universal standards of living. Likewise, outside forces should encourage hydroelectric power plants in the Bosnian Federation to sell electric power to Srpskan heavy industries and refineries. The economic growth should help alleviate tensions between the two ethnic groups.

Fostering increased economic interaction between the Bosnian Federation and the Republika Srpska might make the two quasi states dependent on each other for continued prosperity. This interdependence might in turn make the reintegration and reunification called for by Dayton the result of self-interest rather than foreign imposition.

Given the high potential for gains from economic integration and despite the momentum of the status quo, a no war, no peace scenario is the most likely plight for Bosnia. The policy outcome that corresponds with this scenario is to strengthen informal political autonomy, execute an arms build up for the weaker side, and expedite economic collaboration.

POLITICAL ECONOMY AND PUBLIC OPINION ON KOSOVO

In contrast with Bosnia, it is unlikely that economic integration would result in political cooperation in Kosovo. Following the spring 1999 hostilities, economic gains are not likely to produce political unification of Kosovo with Serbia. Consider the Bosnian-Serb quest for independence in relation to the ethnic Albanian pursuit of limited autonomy or full sovereignty. The provisions of the Dayton

Accords virtually eliminate the possibility of Bosnian Serb sovereignty. Although Western diplomats oppose the Kosovar goal of independence, there is no external accord like Dayton that makes sovereignty a nonstarter. It is conceivable that economic integration among Croats, Muslims, and Serbs might lead to political cooperation, but it is doubtful that such integration involving ethnic Albanians would decrease their search for separation from Serbia.

Before the spring 1999 fighting in Kosovo, there was a link between economic incentives and Serb attitudes toward autonomy for ethnic Albanians. About a third of the Serbs interviewed in a USIA poll supported a degree of autonomy for ethnic Albanians, if it were accompanied by economic incentives. Indeed, some Serbs may be induced to favor autonomy for Kosovo Albanians if the Serbs received economic rewards in exchange for granting Albanian self-rule.[25]

Prior to the 1999 fighting, Serbs believed that Belgrade should grant Kosovo Albanians some degree of self-rule under three conditions. If autonomy would lead to the lifting of international sanctions against Belgrade, these Serbs (36 percent) favored limited independence. But nearly half (45 percent) would have still opposed that outcome. The Serb public (38 percent) also looked favorably on a compromise with Kosovo Albanians if it would have freed resources used to maintain security in Kosovo for economic development. Nearly half, however, (45 percent) would still oppose. And Serbs (35 percent) favor compromise if it would result in increased trade with other countries. Again, almost half (48 percent) would have still opposed.

Again before the fighting escalated, Serbs who looked favorably on compromise paired with economic incentives were more likely to be supporters of parties opposed to Milosevic. Indeed, a majority of Serbs (58 percent) lacked confidence in Milosevic to do what was right for Serbia. There was more support for Bosnian Serb leaders Mladic and Karadzic than for Milosevic. According to a February 1997 USIA poll, the Bosnian Serb leaders had popularity ratings of 90 percent and 85 percent, respectively. A March 1998 USIA poll found that overall opinion of Milosevic was more unfavorable (58 percent) than favorable (39 percent). The 1999 war, however, increased Milosevic's popularity.

While the Kosovars expect autonomy and hope for a referendum that would allow for independence from Belgrade, the Serb public believed that Kosovo is an internal affair. About 90 percent of the Serbs asserted that the situation in Kosovo is strictly the business of Serbia. The Serb public held that neither international organizations nor regional entities should be involved in dispute settlement in Kosovo. They did not favor a role for the United Nations or NATO in Kosovo. In the negotiations during February 1999, Belgrade held that the presence of NATO monitors in Kosovo was a diplomatic nonstarter, and the monitors withdrew when tensions between Belgrade and Brussels escalated in the spring.

Even before the hostilities of 1999, Serbs strongly rejected independence for ethnic Albanians. Indeed, few Serbs (26 percent) favored autonomous status for Kosovo within Serbia. The Serb population (70 percent) even opposed granting limited autonomy over local institutions like municipal government, courts, police, and public transportation. Most Serbs (92 percent) believed the situation in Kosovo was a serious threat. But many Serbs were not willing to sacrifice their own lives in order to keep Kosovo within Serbia. Slightly more Serbs opposed (45 percent) than favored (37 percent) a member of their immediate family deploying to fight in Kosovo to keep it as a part of Serbia. But the hostilities during the spring of 1999 probably increased the proportion of Serbs who would approve of deployment in Kosovo.

In light of this discussion of political economy and public opinion concerning Kosovo, here is a review of objectives, options, scenarios, and outcomes for that province as discussed more fully in the Preface.

OBJECTIVES, OPTIONS, SCENARIOS, AND OUTCOMES FOR KOSOVO

During spring 1999, NATO objectives in Kosovo included destruction, removal, repatriation, and protection. In view of these aims, political and military options facing the alliance consisted of political options—reconciliation, containment, and regime change—as well as military options—airstrikes or a combination of air war and ground combat. The likelihood of each outcome depended on the scenario that unfolded, which in turn followed from the option chosen. Potential scenarios included Serb triumph; standoff, but Serbs dominate; deadlock; stalemate, but NATO dominates; NATO victory.

Following from each scenario were outcomes involving the status of Kosovo and concerning the leadership of Yugoslavia. The possible outcomes for Kosovo were puppet province, partition, Rambouillet, Rambouillet Minus, and Rambouillet Plus. The set of outcomes pertaining to the leadership of Yugoslavia were that Milosevic would retain power on his own terms, that he would remain in control on NATO's terms, that he would be ousted in a coup, or that he would leave office in a peaceful democratic transition.

During the 1999 combat, NATO discussed compromising its aims and entering into a ceasefire, retaining the goals of destruction, removal, repatriation, and protection while intensifying the air war, or broadening the objectives to include overthrow of the regime in Belgrade through a combined air/land battle. Assuming NATO victory and an outcome of Rambouillet Plus, NATO has the opportunity to facilitate collective economic action and the development of shared political institutions throughout the Balkans.

Following World War II, the United States helped Western Europe rebuild its war-torn industries with the Marshall Plan; following the war over Kosovo, there is a need for a new Marshall Plan funded mainly by Western Europe for the purpose of rebuilding the Balkans.

CONCLUSION

A preponderance of power was necessary to bring the parties in the Bosnian conflict to the negotiating table and keep them there; a balance of power among the parties in Bosnia is necessary to keep the peace. Otherwise, the vacuum created by the withdrawal of Western troops may be filled with unprincipled personalities. To avoid recurrence of war in Bosnia, the West would be well advised to understand the role that preponderance-of-power principles played in bringing hostilities to an end in Bosnia. Washington should be especially aware that even if it were no longer part of a military presence in southern Europe, it would still be called on to play the role of the major political and economic balancer in the Balkans.

With respect to Kosovo, even a preponderance of power was insufficient for NATO to bring the parties to the table and coerce them to accept a compromise settlement. Brute force was necessary to degrade Serb military capabilities to the point that Belgrade no longer would pose a threat to its neighbors or to the ethnic Albanians of Kosovo.

Following the 1999 fighting, there is a need for a sustained political and economic commitment to the Balkans by Western Europe. Led by NATO, the European Union, and the Organization for Security and Cooperation in Europe, international bodies need to work in concert to build a warm peace on the ashes of a hot war.

In addition, Washington needs to reward progress in a Balkan peace process the way it reinforces positive behavior in the Arab-Israel peace process. As a result of Camp David and the Israel-Egypt peace treaty, military and economic assistance flowed to the parties. Likewise, the Palestinians receive assistance from Western countries consistent with their participation in peace process. The West, led by the United States, needs to institute a similar system of credible promises in the form of economic rewards in the Balkans. This reward system would complement the threat system that characterized the 1990s.

The system of issuing credible threats and rewards is a central component of the concept of balance of power, which is grounded in the basic concept of deterrence. It manages power and policy situations in a pluralistic world of independent states in such a fashion that potential disturbers of the peace are kept in check by the threat that their trouble-making enterprises will be detected and deterred.

Differences between Moscow and Washington coupled with disputes among the Western allies resulted in the lack of a decisive coalition. Consequently, rogue leaders like Milosevic, Karadzic, and Mladic had free rein to act. They were constrained neither by a regional balance nor by a preponderance of power from the international community.

The local balance in the Balkans gave the "rogues" too much freedom of action, but a preponderance of Western power eventually overwhelmed them. At issue is whether in the absence of dominant Western military capabilities in the region the local balance of power among the parties can suffice to maintain the ceasefire. Those individuals who began the Bosnian war in the first place could fill this void. They must perceive Washington as willing and able to intervene again to maintain the peace. The United States and NATO at the end of the twentieth century can be the holder of the balance in the Balkans, as England was the balancer in nineteenth century Europe.

For progressive economic integration to occur, the issue of potential aggression by any of the parties must be addressed. If a disparity of force exists between the Republika Srpska and the Bosnian Federation, arms control needs to redress the balance. Without steps to equalize the three ethnic actors, those parties that feel threatened will begin to operate from a basement of fear once again. Engaging fearful parties may require arming the weakest.

In summary, the Dayton Peace Agreement and nascent peace accords for Kosovo seek to move from combat via coercion to commerce. Economic gain through commerce for each might be a selective incentive for the ethnic groups to cooperate for the sake of the collective good. Commerce would lessen the effect of ethnic differences, but not eliminate them. Meanwhile, coercion and brute force continue to play a role in gaining the compliance of the ethnic groups. In this respect, military power may facilitate a transition from tribalization to globalization.

APPENDIX

BALANCING IN THE BALKANS

GENERAL FRAMEWORK AGREEMENT FOR PEACE IN BOSNIA AND HERZEGOVINA

The Republic of Bosnia and Herzegovina, the Republic of Croatia and the Federal Republic of Yugoslavia (the " Parties"),

Recognizing the need for a comprehensive settlement to bring an end to the tragic conflict in the region,
Desiring to contribute toward that end and to promote an enduring peace and stability,

Affirming their commitment to the Agreed Basic Principles issued on September 8, 1995, the Further Agreed Basic Principles issued on September 26, 1995, and the cease–fire agreements of September 14 and October 5, 1995,

Noting the agreement of August 29, 1995, which authorized the delegation of the Federal Republic of Yugoslavia to sign, on behalf of the Republika Srpska, the parts of the peace plan concerning it, with the obligation to implement the agreement that is reached strictly and consequently,

Have agreed as follows:

Article I:

The Parties shall conduct their relations in accordance with the principles set forth in the United Nations Charter, as well as the Helsinki Final Act and other documents of the Organization for Security and Cooperation in Europe. In particular, the Parties shall fully respect the sovereign equality of one another, shall settle disputes by peaceful means, and shall refrain from any action, by threat or use of force or otherwise, against the territorial integrity or political independence of Bosnia and Herzegovina or any other State.

Article II:

The Parties welcome and endorse the arrangements that have been made concerning the military aspects of the peace settlement and aspects of regional stabilization, as set forth in the Agreements at Annex 1–A and Annex 1–B. The Parties shall fully respect and promote fulfillment of the commitments made in Annex 1–A, and shall comply fully with their commitments as set forth in Annex 1–B.

Article III:

The Parties welcome and endorse the arrangements that have been made concerning the boundary demarcation between the two Entities, the Federation of Bosnia and Herzegovina and Republika Srpska, as set forth in the

Agreement at Annex 2. The Parties shall fully respect and promote fulfillment of the commitments made therein.

Article IV:

The Parties welcome and endorse the elections program for Bosnia and Herzegovina as set forth in Annex 3. The Parties shall fully respect and promote fulfillment of that program.

Article V:

The Parties welcome and endorse the arrangements that have been made concerning the Constitution of Bosnia and Herzegovina, as set forth in Annex 4. The Parties shall fully respect and promote fulfillment of the commitments made therein.

Article VI:

The Parties welcome and endorse the arrangements that have been made concerning the establishment of an arbitration tribunal, a Commission on Human Rights, a Commission on Refugees and Displaced Persons, a Commission to Preserve National Monuments, and Bosnia and Herzegovina Public Corporations, as set forth in the Agreements at Annexes 5–9. The Parties shall fully respect and promote fulfillment of the commitments made therein.

Article VII:

Recognizing that the observance of human rights and the protection of refugees and displaced persons are of vital importance in achieving a lasting peace, the Parties agree to and shall comply fully with the provisions concerning human rights set forth in Chapter One of the Agreement at Annex 6, as well as the provisions concerning refugees and displaced persons set forth in Chapter One of the Agreement at Annex 7.

Article VIII:

The Parties welcome and endorse the arrangements that have been made concerning the implementation of this peace settlement, including in particular those pertaining to the civilian (non–military) implementation, as set forth in the Agreement at Annex 10, and the international police task force, as set forth in the Agreement at Annex 11. The Parties shall fully respect and promote fulfillment of the commitments made therein.

Article IX:

The Parties shall cooperate fully with all entities involved in implementation of this peace settlement, as described in the Annexes to this Agreement, or which are otherwise authorized by the United Nations Security Council, pursuant to the obligation of all Parties to cooperate in the investigation and prosecution of war crimes and other violations of international humanitarian law.

Article X:

The Federal Republic of Yugoslavia and the Republic of Bosnia and Herzegovina recognize each other as sovereign independent States within their international borders. Further aspects of their mutual recognition will be subject to subsequent discussions.

Article XI:

This Agreement shall enter into force upon signature.
DONE at Paris, this [21st] day of [November], 1995, in the Bosnian, Croatian, English and Serbian languages, each text being equally authentic.

    For the Republic of Bosnia and Herzegovina
    For the Republic of Croatia
    For the Federal Republic of Yugoslavia

Witnessed by:

European Union Special Negotiator
For the French Republic
For the Federal Republic of Germany
For the Russian Federation
For the United Kingdom of Great Britain and Northern Ireland
For the United States of America

UNITED NATIONS SECURITY COUNCIL RESOLUTION 713

Adopted by the Security Council at its 3009th meeting, on 25 September 1991 the Security Council,
Conscious of the fact that Yugoslavia has welcomed the convening of a Security Council meeting through a letter conveyed by the Permanent Representative of Yugoslavia to the President of the Security Council (S/23069),
Having heard the statement by the Foreign Minister of Yugoslavia, Deeply concerned by the fighting in Yugoslavia which is causing a heavy loss of human life and material damage, and by the consequences for the countries of the region, in particular in the border areas of neighbouring countries,
Concerned that the continuation of this situation constitutes a threat to international peace and security,
Recalling its primary responsibility under the Charter of the United Nations for the maintenance of international peace and security,
Recalling also the provisions of Chapter VIII of the Charter of the United Nations,
Commending the efforts undertaken by the European Community and its member States, with the support of the States participating in the Conference on Security and Cooperation in Europe, to restore peace and dialogue in Yugoslavia, through, inter alia, the implementation of a cease–fire including the sending of observers, the convening of a Conference on Yugoslavia, including the mechanisms set forth within it, and the suspension of the delivery of all weapons and military equipment to Yugoslavia,
Recalling the relevant principles enshrined in the Charter of the United Nations and, in this context, noting the Declaration of 3 September 1991 of the States participating in the Conference on Security and Cooperation in

Europe that no territorial gains or changes within Yugoslavia brought about by violence are acceptable,

Noting also the agreement for a cease–fire concluded on 17 September 1991 in Igalo, and also that signed on 22 September 1991,

Alarmed by the violations of the cease–fire and the continuation of the fighting,

Taking note of the letter dated 19 September 1991 to the President of the Security Council from the Permanent Representative of Austria (S/23052),

Taking note also of the letters dated 19 September 1991 and 20 September 1991 to the President of the Security Council from respectively the Permanent Representative of Canada (S/23053) and the Permanent Representative of Hungary (S/23057),

Taking note also of the letters dated 5 July 1991 (S/22775), 12 July 1991 (S/22785), 22 July 1991 (S/22834), 6 August 1991 (S/22898), 7 August 1991 (S/22902), 7 August 1991 (S/22903), 21 August 1991 (S/22975), 29 August 1991 (S/22991), 4 September 1991 (S/23010), 19 September 1991 (S/23047), 20 September 1991 (S/23059) and 20 September 1991 (S/23060), from respectively the Permanent Representative of the Netherlands, the Permanent Representative of Czechoslovakia, the Permanent Representatives of Belgium, France and the United Kingdom of Great Britain and Northern Ireland, the Charge d'Affaires a.i. of Austria, and the Permanent Representative of Australia,

Expresses its full support for the collective efforts for peace and dialogue in Yugoslavia undertaken under the auspices of the member States of the European Community with the support of the States participating in the Conference on Security and Cooperation in Europe consistent with the principles of that Conference;

Supports fully all arrangements and measures resulting from such collective efforts as those described above, in particular of assistance and support to the cease–fire observers, to consolidate an effective end to hostilities in Yugoslavia and the smooth functioning of the process instituted within the framework of the Conference on Yugoslavia;

Invites to this end the Secretary–General to offer his assistance without delay, in consultation with the Government of Yugoslavia and all those promoting the efforts referred to above, and to report as soon as possible to the Security Council;

Strongly urges all parties to abide strictly by the cease–fire agreements of 17 September 1991 and 22 September 1991;

Appeals urgently to and encourages all parties to settle their disputes peacefully and through negotiation at the Conference on Yugoslavia, including through the mechanisms set forth within it;

Decides, under Chapter VII of the Charter of the United Nations, that all States shall, for the purposes of establishing peace and stability in Yugoslavia, immediately implement a general and complete embargo on all deliveries of weapons and military equipment to Yugoslavia until the Security Council decides otherwise following consultation between the Secretary–General and the Government of Yugoslavia;

Calls on all States to refrain from any action which might contribute to increasing tension and to impeding or delaying a peaceful and negotiated outcome to the conflict in Yugoslavia, which would permit all Yugoslavs to decide upon and to construct their future in peace;

Decides to remain seized of the matter until a peaceful solution is achieved.

UNITED NATIONS SECURITY COUNCIL RESOLUTION 743

Adopted by the Security Council at its 3055th meeting, on 21 February 1992 the Security Council,

Reaffirming its resolutions 713 (1991) of 25 September 1991, 721 (1991) of 27 November 1991, 724 (1991) of 15 December 1991, 727 (1992) of 8 January 1992 and 740 (1992) of 7 February 1992,

Noting the report of the Secretary–General of 15 February 1992 (S/23592) submitted pursuant to resolution 721 (1991), and the request of the Government of Yugoslavia (S/23240) for a peace–keeping operation referred to in that resolution,

Noting in particular that the Secretary–General considers that the conditions permitting the early deployment of a United Nations Protection Force (UNPROFOR) are met and welcoming his recommendation that this Force should be established with immediate effect,

Expressing its gratitude to the Secretary–General and his Personal Envoy for their contribution to the achievement of conditions facilitating the deployment of a United Nations Protection Force (UNPROFOR) and their continuing commitment to this effort,

Concerned that the situation in Yugoslavia continues to constitute a threat to international peace and security, as determined in resolution 713 (1991),

Recalling its primary responsibility under the Charter of the United Nations for the maintenance of international peace and security,

Recalling also the provisions of Article 25 Chapter VIII of the Charter of the United Nations,

Commending again the efforts undertaken by the European Community and its member States, with the support of the States participating in the

Conference on Security and Cooperation in Europe, through the convening of a Conference on Yugoslavia, including the mechanisms set forth within it, to ensure a peaceful political settlement,

Convinced that the implementation of the United Nations peace–keeping plan (S/23280, annex III) will assist the Conference on Yugoslavia in reaching a peaceful political settlement,

Approves the report of the Secretary–General of 15 February 1992 (S/23592);

Decides to establish, under its authority, a United Nations Protection Force (UNPROFOR) in accordance with the above–mentioned report and the United Nations peace–keeping plan and requests the Secretary–General to take the measures necessary to ensure its earliest possible deployment;

Decides that, in order to implement the recommendations in paragraph 30 of the report of the Secretary–General, the Force is established in accordance with paragraph 4 below, for an initial period of 12 months unless the Council subsequently decides otherwise;

Requests the Secretary–General immediately to deploy those elements of the Force which can assist in developing an implementation plan for the earliest possible full deployment of the force for approval by the Council and a budget which together will maximize the contribution of the Yugoslav parties to offsetting its costs and in all other ways secure the most efficient and cost–effective operation possible;

Recalls that, in accordance with paragraph 1 of the United Nations peace–keeping plan, the Force should be an interim arrangement to create the conditions of peace and security required for the negotiation of an overall settlement of the Yugoslav crisis;

Invites accordingly the Secretary–General to report as appropriate and not less than every six months on progress towards a peaceful political settlement and the situation on the ground, and to submit a first report on the establishment of the Force within two months of the adoption of this resolution;

Undertakes, in this connection, to examine without delay any recommendations that the Secretary–General may make in his reports concerning the Force, including the duration of its mission, and to adopt appropriate decisions;

Urges all parties and others concerned to comply strictly with the cease–fire arrangements signed at Geneva on 23 November 1991 and at Sarajevo on 2 January 1992, and to cooperate fully and unconditionally in the implementation of the peace–keeping plan;

Demands that all parties and others concerned take all the necessary measures to ensure the safety of the personnel sent by the United Nations and of the members of the European Community Monitoring Mission;

Calls again upon the Yugoslav parties to cooperate fully with the Conference on Yugoslavia in its aim of reaching a political settlement consistent with the principles of the Conference on Security and Cooperation in Europe and reaffirms that the United Nations peace–keeping plan and its implementation is in no way intended to prejudge the terms of a political settlement;

Decides within the same framework that the embargo imposed by paragraph 6 of Security Council resolution 713 (1991) shall not apply to weapons and military equipment destined for the sole use of UNPROFOR;

Requests all States to provide appropriate support to UNPROFOR, in particular to permit and facilitate the transit of its personnel and equipment;

Decides to remain actively seized of the matter until a peaceful solution is achieved.

UNITED NATIONS SECURITY COUNCIL RESOLUTION 836

Adopted by the Security Council at its 3228th meeting, on 4 June 1993 the Security Council,

Reaffirming its resolution 713 (1991) of 25 September 1991 and all subsequent relevant resolutions,

Reaffirming in particular its resolutions 819 (1993) of 16 April 1993 and 824 (1993) of 6 May 1993, which demanded that certain towns and their surrounding areas in the Republic of Bosnia and Herzegovina should be treated as safe areas,

Reaffirming the sovereignty, territorial integrity and political independence of the Republic of Bosnia and Herzegovina and the responsibility of the Security Council in this regard,

Condemning military attacks, and actions that do not respect the sovereignty, territorial integrity and political independence of the Republic of Bosnia and Herzegovina, which, as a State Member of the United Nations, enjoys the rights provided for in the Charter of the United Nations, Reiterating its alarm at the grave and intolerable situation in the Republic of Bosnia and Herzegovina arising from serious violations of international humanitarian law,

Reaffirming once again that any taking of territory by force or any practice of "ethnic cleansing" is unlawful and totally unacceptable,

Commending the Government of the Republic of Bosnia and Herzegovina and the Bosnian Croat party for having signed the Vance–Owen Plan,

Gravely concerned at the persistent refusal of the Bosnian Serb party to accept the Vance–Owen Plan and calling upon that party to accept the Peace Plan for the Republic of Bosnia and Herzegovina in full,

Deeply concerned by the continuing armed hostilities in the territory of the Republic of Bosnia and Herzegovina which run totally counter to the Peace Plan,

Alarmed by the resulting plight of the civilian population in the territory of the Republic of Bosnia and Herzegovina in particular in Sarajevo, Bihac, Srebrenica, Gorazde, Tuzla and Zepa,

Condemning the obstruction, primarily by the Bosnian Serb party, of the delivery of humanitarian assistance,

Determined to ensure the protection of the civilian population in safe areas and to promote a lasting political solution,

Confirming the ban on military flights in the airspace of the Republic of Bosnia and Herzegovina, established by resolutions 781 (1992) of 9 October 1992, 786 (1992) of 10 November 1992 and 816 (1993) of 31 March 1993, Affirming that the concept of safe areas in the Republic of Bosnia and Herzegovina as contained in resolutions 819 (1993) and 824 (1993) was adopted to respond to an emergency situation, and noting that the concept proposed by France in document S/25800 and by others could make a valuable contribution and should not in any way be taken as an end in itself, but as part of the Vance–Owen process and as a first step towards a just and lasting political solution,

Convinced that treating the towns and surrounding areas referred to above as safe areas will contribute to the early implementation of that objective,

Stressing that the lasting solution to the conflict in the Republic of Bosnia and Herzegovina must be based on the following principles: immediate and complete cessation of hostilities; withdrawal from territories seized by the use of force and "ethnic cleansing;" reversal of the consequences of "ethnic cleansing" and recognition of the right of all refugees to return to their homes; and respect for sovereignty, territorial integrity and political independence of the Republic of Bosnia and Herzegovina,

Noting also the crucial work being done throughout the Republic of Bosnia and Herzegovina by the United Nations Protection Force (UNPROFOR), and the importance of such work continuing,

Determining that the situation in the Republic of Bosnia and Herzegovina continues to be a threat to international peace and security, Acting under Chapter VII of the Charter of the United Nations,

Calls for the full and immediate implementation of all its relevant resolutions;

Commends the Peace Plan for the Republic of Bosnia and Herzegovina as contained in document S/25479);

Reaffirms the unacceptability of the acquisition of territory by the use of force and the need to restore the full sovereignty, territorial integrity and political independence of the Republic of Bosnia and Herzegovina,

Decides to ensure full respect for the safe areas referred to in resolution 824 (1993);

Decides to extend to that end the mandate of UNPROFOR in order to enable it, in the safe areas referred to in resolution 824 (1993), to deter attacks against the safe areas, to monitor the cease–fire, to promote the withdrawal of military or paramilitary units other than those of the Government of the Republic of Bosnia and Herzegovina and to occupy some key points on the ground, in addition to participating in the delivery of humanitarian relief to the population as provided for in resolution 776 (1992) of 14 September 1992,

Affirms that these safe areas are a temporary measure and that the primary objective remains to reverse the consequences of the use of force and to allow all persons displaced from their homes in the Republic of Bosnia and Herzegovina to return to their homes in peace, beginning, inter alia, with the prompt implementation of the provisions of the Vance–Owen Plan in areas where those have been agreed by the parties directly concerned;

Requests the Secretary–General, in consultation, inter alia, with the Governments of the Member States contributing forces to UNPROFOR: (a) To make the adjustments or reinforcement of UNPROFOR which might be required by the implementation of the present resolution, and to consider assigning UNPROFOR elements in support of the elements entrusted with protection of safe areas, with the agreement of the Governments contributing forces; (b) To direct the UNPROFOR Force Commander to redeploy to the extent possible the forces under his command in the Republic of Bosnia and Herzegovina;

Calls upon Member States to contribute forces, including logistic support, to facilitate the implementation of the provisions regarding the safe areas, expresses its gratitude to Members States already providing forces for that purpose and invites the Secretary–General to seek additional contingents from other Member States;

Authorizes UNPROFOR, in addition to the mandate defined in resolutions 770 (1992) of 13 August 1992 and 776 (1992), in carrying out the mandate defined in paragraph 5 above, acting in self–defence, to take the necessary measures, including the use of force, in reply to bombardments against the safe areas by any of the parties or to armed incursion into them or in the event of any deliberate obstruction in or around those areas to the freedom of movement of UNPROFOR or of protected humanitarian convoys;

Decides that, notwithstanding paragraph 1 of resolution 816 (1993), Member States, acting nationally or through regional organizations or arrangements, may take, under the authority of the Security Council and subject to close coordination with the Secretary–General and UNPROFOR, all necessary measures, through the use of air power, in and around the safe areas in the Republic of Bosnia and Herzegovina, to support UNPROFOR in the performance of its mandate set out in paragraph 5 and 9 above;

Request the Members States concerned, the Secretary–General and UNPROFOR to coordinate closely on the measures they are taking to implement paragraph 10 above and to report to the Council through the Secretary–General;

Invites the Secretary–General to report to the Council, for decision, if possible within seven days of the adoption of the present resolution, on the modalities of its implementation, including its financial implications;

Further invites the Secretary–General to submit to the Council, not later than two months after the adoption of the present resolution, a report on the implementation of and compliance with the present resolution;

Emphasizes that it will keep open other options for new and tougher measures, none of which is prejudged or excluded from consideration;

Decides to remain actively seized of the matter, and undertakes to take prompt action, as required.

UNITED NATIONS SECURITY COUNCIL RESOLUTION 838

Adopted by the Security Council at its 3234th meeting, on 10 June 1993 the Security Council,

Reaffirming its resolution 713 (1991) of 25 September 1991 and all subsequent relevant resolutions,

Reaffirming the sovereignty, territorial integrity and political independence of the Republic of Bosnia and Herzegovina and the responsibility of the Security Council in this regard,

Reiterating the demands in its resolution 752 (1992) and subsequent relevant resolutions that all forms of interference from outside the Republic of Bosnia and Herzegovina cease immediately and that its neighbours take swift action to end all interference and respect its territorial integrity, Recalling the demand in its resolution 819 (1993) that the Federal Republic of

Yugoslavia (Serbia and Montenegro) immediately cease the supply of military arms, equipment and services to Bosnian Serb paramilitary units, Taking into account the report of the Secretary–General dated 21 December 1992 (S/25000) on the possible deployment of observers on the borders of the Republic of Bosnia and Herzegovina,

Expressing its condemnation of all activities carried out in violation of resolutions 757 (1992), 787 (1992) and 820 (1993) between the territory of the Federal Republic of Yugoslavia (Serbia and Montenegro) and the United Nations Protected Areas in the Republic of Croatia and those areas of the Republic of Bosnia and Herzegovina under the control of Bosnian Serb forces,

Considering that, in order to facilitate the implementation of the relevant Security Council resolutions, observers should be deployed on the borders of the Republic of Bosnia and Herzegovina, as indicated in its resolution 787 (1992),

Taking note of the earlier preparedness of the authorities in the Federal Republic of Yugoslavia (Serbia and Montenegro) to stop all but humanitarian supplies to the Bosnian Serb party, and urging full implementation of that commitment,

Considering that all appropriate measures should be undertaken to achieve a peaceful settlement of the conflict in the Republic of Bosnia and Herzegovina provided for in the Vance–Owen Peace Plan,

Bearing in mind paragraph 4 (a) of its resolution 757 (1992) concerning the prevention by all States of imports into their territories of all commodities and products originating in or exported from the Federal Republic of Yugoslavia (Serbia and Montenegro) and paragraph 12 of its resolution 820 (1993) concerning import to, export from and transshipment through those areas of the Republic of Bosnia and Herzegovina under the control of the Bosnian Serb forces,

1.   Requests the Secretary–General to submit to the Council as soon as possible a further report on options for the deployment of international observers to monitor effectively the implementation of the relevant Security Council resolutions, to be drawn from the United Nations and, if appropriate, from Member States acting nationally or through regional organizations and arrangements, on the borders of the Republic of Bosnia and Herzegovina, giving priority to the border between the Republic of Bosnia and Herzegovina and the Federal Republic of Yugoslavia (Serbia and Montenegro) and taking into account developments since his report of 21 December 1992 as well as

the differing circumstances affecting the various sectors of the borders and the need for appropriate coordination mechanisms;

2. Invites the Secretary–General to contact immediately Member States, nationally or through regional organizations or arrangements, to ensure the availability to him on a continuing basis of any relevant material derived from aerial surveillance and to report thereon to the Security Council;

3. Decides to remain seized of the matter.

UNITED NATIONS SECURITY COUNCIL RESOLUTION 843

Adopted by the Security Council at its 3240th meeting, on 18 June 1993 the Security Council,

Recalling its resolution 724 (1991) concerning Yugoslavia and all other relevant resolutions,

Recalling also Article 50 of the Charter of the United Nations,

Conscious of the fact that an increasing number of requests for assistance have been received under the provisions of Article 50 of the Charter of the United Nations,

Noting that the Security Council Committee established pursuant to resolution 724 (1991), at its 65th meeting, set up a working group to examine the above–mentioned requests,

Confirms that the Committee established pursuant to resolution 724 (1991) is entrusted with the task of examining requests for assistance under the provisions of Article 50 of the Charter of the United Nations;

Welcomes the establishment by the Committee of its working group and invites the Committee, as it completes the examination of each request, to make recommendations to the President of the Security Council for appropriate action.

UNITED NATIONS SECURITY COUNCIL RESOLUTION 844

Adopted by the Security Council at its 3241st meeting, on 18 June 1993 the Security Council,

Reaffirming its resolution 713 (1991) of 25 September 1991 and all subsequent relevant resolutions,

Having considered the report of the Secretary–General (S/25939 and Corr.1 and Add.1) pursuant to paragraph 12 of resolution 836 (1993) concerning the safe areas in the Republic of Bosnia and Herzegovina,

Reiterating once again its alarm at the grave and intolerable situation in the Republic of Bosnia and Herzegovina arising from serious violations of international humanitarian law,

Recalling the overwhelming importance of seeking a comprehensive political solution to the conflict in the Republic of Bosnia and Herzegovina,

Determined to implement fully the provisions of resolution 836 (1993),

Acting under Chapter VII of the Charter of the United Nations,

1. Approves the report of the Secretary–General;
2. Decides to authorize the reinforcement of the United Nations Protection
3. Force (UNPROFOR) to meet the additional force requirements mentioned in paragraph 6 of the report of the Secretary–General;
4. Requests the Secretary–General to continue the consultations, inter alia, with the Governments of the Member States contributing forces to UNPROFOR, called for in resolution 836 (1993);
5. Reaffirms its decision in paragraph 10 of resolution 836 (1993) on the use of air power, in and around the safe areas, to support UNPROFOR in the performance of its mandate, and encourages Member States, acting nationally or through regional organizations or arrangements, to coordinate closely with the Secretary–General in this regard;
6. Calls upon Member States to contribute forces, including logistic support and equipment to facilitate the implementation of the provisions regarding the safe areas;
7. Invites the Secretary–General to report to the Council on a regular basis on the implementation of resolution 836 (1993) and this resolution;
8. Decides to remain actively seized of the matter.

UNITED NATIONS SECURITY COUNCIL RESOLUTION 1160

Adopted by the Security Council at its 3868th meeting, on 31 March 1998 the Security Council,

Not with appreciation the statements of the Foreign Ministers of France, Germany, Italy, the Russian Federation, the United Kingdom of Great Britain and Northern Ireland and the United States of America (the Contact Group) of 9 and 25 March 1998 (S/1998/223 and S/1998/272), including the proposal on a comprehensive arms embargo on the Federal Republic of Yugoslavia, including Kosovo,

Welcoming the decision of the Special Session of the Permanent Council of the Organization for Security and Cooperation in Europe (OSCE) of 11 March 1998 (S/1998/246),

Condemning the use of excessive force by Serbian police forces against civilians and peaceful demonstrators in Kosovo, as well as all acts of terrorism by the Kosovo Liberation Army or any other group or individual and all external support for terrorist activity in Kosovo, including finance, arms and training,

Noting the declaration of 18 March 1998 by the President of the Republic of Serbia on the political process in Kosovo and Metohija (S/1998/250),

Noting also the clear commitment of senior representatives of the Kosovar Albanian community to non–violence,

Noting that there has been some progress in implementing the actions indicated in the Contact Group statement of 9 March 1998, but stressing that further progress is required,

Affirming the commitment of all Member States to the sovereignty and territorial integrity of the Federal Republic of Yugoslavia,

Acting under Chapter VII of the Charter of the United Nations,

1. Calls upon the Federal Republic of Yugoslavia immediately to take the further necessary steps to achieve a political solution to the issue of Kosovo through dialogue and to implement the actions indicated in the Contact Group statements of 9 and 25 March 1998;

2. Calls also upon the Kosovar Albanian leadership to condemn all terrorist action, and emphasizes that all elements in the Kosovar Albanian community should pursue their goals by peaceful means only;

3. Underlines that the way to defeat violence and terrorism in Kosovo is for the authorities in Belgrade to offer the Kosovar Albanian community a genuine political process;

4. Calls upon the authorities in Belgrade and the leadership of the Kosovar Albanian community urgently to enter without preconditions into a meaningful dialogue on political status issues, and notes the readiness of the Contact Group to facilitate such a dialogue;

5. Agrees, without prejudging the outcome of that dialogue, with the proposal in the Contact Group statements of 9 and 25 March 1998

that the principles for a solution of the Kosovo problem should be based on the territorial integrity of the Federal Republic of Yugoslavia and should be in accordance with OSCE standards, including those set out in the Helsinki Final Act of the Conference on Security and Cooperation in Europe of 1975, and the Charter of the United Nations, and that such a solution must also take into account the rights of the Kosovar Albanians and all who live in Kosovo, and expresses its support for an enhanced status for Kosovo which would include a substantially greater degree of autonomy and meaningful self–administration;

6. Welcomes the signature on 23 March 1998 of an agreement on measures to implement the 1996 Education Agreement, calls upon all parties to ensure that its implementation proceeds smoothly and without delay according to the agreed timetable and expresses its readiness to consider measures if either party blocks implementation;

7. Expresses its support for the efforts of the OSCE for a peaceful resolution of the crisis in Kosovo, including through the Personal Representative of the Chairman–in–Office for the Federal Republic of Yugoslavia, who is also the Special Representative of the European Union, and the return of the OSCE long–term missions;

8. Decides that all States shall, for the purposes of fostering peace and stability in Kosovo, prevent the sale or supply to the Federal Republic of Yugoslavia, including Kosovo, by their nationals or from their territories or using their flag vessels and aircraft, of arms and related materiel of all types, such as weapons and ammunition, military vehicles and equipment and spare parts for the aforementioned, and shall prevent arming and training for terrorist activities there;

9. Decides to establish, in accordance with rule 28 of its provisional rules of procedure, a committee of the Security Council, consisting of all the members of the Council, to undertake the following tasks and to report on its work to the Council with its observations and recommendations: (a) to seek from all States information regarding the action taken by them concerning the effective implementation of the prohibitions imposed by this resolution; (b) to consider any information brought to its attention by any State concerning violations of the prohibitions imposed by this resolution and to recommend appropriate measures in response thereto; (c) to make periodic reports to the Security Council on information submitted to it regarding alleged violations of the prohibitions imposed by this resolution; (d) to promulgate such guidelines as may be necessary to facilitate the

implementation of the prohibitions imposed by this resolution; (e) to examine the reports submitted pursuant to paragraph 12 below;

10. Calls upon all States and all international and regional organizations to act strictly in conformity with this resolution, notwithstanding the existence of any rights granted or obligations conferred or imposed by any international agreement or of any contract entered into or any license or permit granted prior to the entry into force of the prohibitions imposed by this resolution, and stresses in this context the importance of continuing implementation of the Agreement on Subregional Arms Control signed in Florence on 14 June 1996;

11. Requests the Secretary–General to provide all necessary assistance to the committee established by paragraph 9 above and to make the necessary arrangements in the Secretariat for this purpose;

12. Requests States to report to the committee established by paragraph 9 above within 30 days of adoption of this resolution on the steps they have taken to give effect to the prohibitions imposed by this resolution;

13. Invites the OSCE to keep the Secretary–General informed on the situation in Kosovo and on measures taken by that organization in this regard;

14. Requests the Secretary–General to keep the Council regularly informed and to report on the situation in Kosovo and the implementation of this resolution no later than 30 days following the adoption of this resolution and every 30 days thereafter;

15. Further requests that the Secretary–General, in consultation with appropriate regional organizations, include in his first report recommendations for the establishment of a comprehensive regime to monitor the implementation of the prohibitions imposed by this resolution, and calls upon all States, in particular neighbouring States, to extend full cooperation in this regard;

16. Decides to review the situation on the basis of the reports of the Secretary–General, which will take into account the assessments of, inter alia, the Contact Group, the OSCE and the European union, and decides also to reconsider the prohibitions imposed by this resolution, including action to terminate them, following receipt of the assessment of the Secretary–General that the Government of the Federal Republic of Yugoslavia, cooperating in a constructive manner with the Contact Group, have: (a) begun a substantive dialogue in accordance with paragraph 4 above, including the participation of an outside representative or representatives, unless

any failure to do so is not because of the position of the Federal Republic of Yugoslavia or Serbian authorities; (b) withdrawn the special police units and ceased action by the security forces affecting the civilian population; (c) allowed access to Kosovo by humanitarian organizations as well as representatives of Contact Group and other embassies; (d) accepted a mission by the Personal Representative of the OSCE Chairman–in–Office for the Federal Republic of Yugoslavia that would include a new and specific mandate for addressing the problems in Kosovo, as well as the return of the OSCE long–term missions; (e) facilitated a mission to Kosovo by the United Nations High Commissioner for Human Rights;

17. Urges the Office of the Prosecutor of the International Tribunal established pursuant to resolution 827 (1993) of 25 May 1993 to begin gathering information related to the violence in Kosovo that may fall within its jurisdiction, and notes that the authorities of the Federal Republic of Yugoslavia have an obligation to cooperate with the Tribunal and that the Contact Group countries will make available to the Tribunal substantiated relevant information in their possession;

18. Affirms that concrete progress to resolve the serious political and human rights issues in Kosovo will improve the international position of the Federal Republic of Yugoslavia and prospects for normalization of its international relationships and full participation in international institutions;

19. Emphasizes that failure to make constructive progress towards the peaceful resolution of the situation in Kosovo will lead to the consideration of additional measures;

20. Decides to remain seized of the matter.

UNITED NATIONS SECURITY COUNCIL RESOLUTION 1168

Adopted by the Security Council at its 3883rd meeting, on 21 May 1998 the Security Council,

Recalling all its previous relevant resolutions concerning the conflicts in the former Yugoslavia, including resolutions 1031 (1995) of 15 December 1995, 1035 (1995) of 21 December 1995, 1088 (1996) of 12 December 1996, 1103 (1997) of 31 March 1997, 1107 (1997) of 16 May 1997 and 1144 (1997) of 19 December 1997,

Expressing its continued commitment to the political settlement of conflicts in the former Yugoslavia, preserving the sovereignty and territorial integrity of all States there within their internationally recognized borders,

Recalling the conclusions of the Steering Board of the Peace Implementation Council held in Sintra on 30 May 1997 (S/1997/434, annex) and the Peace Implementation Conference held in Bonn on 9 and 10 December 1997 (S/1997/979, annex),

Having considered the report of the Secretary–General of 12 March 1998 (S/1998/227 and Add.1), and taking note of his observations and the planning outlined in paragraphs 37 to 46 of that report,

Reaffirming its full support for the High Representative and his staff and his responsibility in implementing the civilian aspects of the General Framework Agreement for Peace in Bosnia and Herzegovina and the Annexes thereto (collectively the Peace Agreement, S/1995/999, annex),

Commending the United Nations mission in Bosnia and Herzegovina (UNMIBH), including the international Police Task Force (IPTF), and recalling the recommendations of the Bonn Peace Implementation Conference relating to UNMIBH, including the IPTF,

Expressing its appreciation to the personnel of UNMIBH, including the IPTF, and to the Special Representative of the Secretary–General and the IPTF commissioner,

Emphasizing the increasing importance of specialized training for local police in Bosnia and Herzegovina, especially in the areas of critical incident management, corruption, organized crime and drug control, as outlined in the report of the Secretary–General,

Acknowledging that success in the area of police reform in Bosnia and Herzegovina is closely linked to complementary judicial reform, and taking note of the report of the High Representative of 9 April 1998 (S/1998/314), which emphasizes that judicial reform is a priority for further progress,

1. Decides to authorize an increase in the strength of the IPTF by 30 posts, to a total authorized strength of 2,057;

2. Supports the improvements in the overall management of the IPTF undertaken by the Secretary–General, his special Representatives, and the IPTF Commissioners and personnel in Bosnia and Herzegovina, stresses the importance of continued reforms in this area, and in this regard strongly encourages the Secretary–General to make further improvements to the IPTF, in particular with regard to personnel management issues;

3.   Encourages Member States to intensify their efforts to provide, on a voluntary funded basis and in coordination with the IPTF, training, equipment and related assistance for local police forces in Bosnia and Herzegovina;

4.   Recognizes that establishing an indigenous public security capability is essential to strengthening the rule of law in Bosnia and Herzegovina, agrees to consider expeditiously an UNMIBH-led court monitoring programme as part of an overall programme of legal reform as outlined by the office of the High Representative, and requests the Secretary–General to submit recommendations on the possibility of utilizing locally hired personnel as far as is practical and of voluntary funding;

5.   Decides to remain seized of the matter.

UNITED NATIONS SECURITY COUNCIL RESOLUTION 1174

Adopted by the Security Council at its 3892nd meeting, on 15 June 1998
The Security Council,
Recalling all its previous relevant resolutions concerning the conflicts in the former Yugoslavia, including resolutions 1031 (1995) of 15 December 1995, 1035 (1995) of 21 December 1995, 1088 (1996) of 12 December 1996, 1144 (1997) of 19 December 1997 and 1168 (1998) of 21 May 1998,
Reaffirming its commitment to the political settlement of the conflicts in the former Yugoslavia, preserving the sovereignty and territorial integrity of all States there within their internationally recognized borders,
Underlining its commitment to supporting implementation of the General Framework Agreement for Peace in Bosnia and Herzegovina and the Annexes thereto (collectively the Peace Agreement, S/1995/999, annex),
Emphasizing its appreciation to the High Representative, the Commander and personnel of the multinational stabilization force (SFOR), the Special Representative of the Secretary–General and the personnel of the United Nations mission in Bosnia and Herzegovina (UNMIBH) including the Commissioner and personnel of the International Police Task Force (IPTF), and the personnel of other international organizations and agencies in Bosnia and Herzegovina for their contributions to the implementation of the Peace Agreement,

Underlining once again the important role for the Republic of Croatia and the Federal Republic of Yugoslavia to play in the successful development of the peace process in Bosnia and Herzegovina,

Stressing that a comprehensive and coordinated return of refugees and displaced persons throughout the region is crucial to lasting peace,

Taking note of the declaration of the Peace Implementation Council Steering Board in Luxembourg on 9 June 1998 (S/1998/498, annex) and the conclusions of its previous meetings,

Having considered the report of the Secretary–General of 10 June 1998 (S/1998/491),

Noting the report of the High Representative of 9 April 1998 (S/1998/314),

Determining that the situation in the region continues to constitute a threat to international peace and security,

Determined to promote the peaceful resolution of the conflicts in accordance with the purposes and principles of the Charter of the United Nations,

Acting under Chapter VII of the Charter of the United Nations,

I

1. Reaffirms once again its support for the Peace Agreement, as well as for the Dayton Agreement on implementing the Federation of Bosnia and Herzegovina of 10 November 1995 (S/1995/1021, annex), calls upon the parties to comply strictly with their obligations under those Agreements, and expresses its intention to keep the implementation of the Peace Agreement, and the situation in Bosnia and Herzegovina under review;

2. Reiterates that the primary responsibility for the further successful implementation of the peace process lies with the authorities in Bosnia and Herzegovina themselves and that the continued willingness of the international community and major donors to assume the political, military and economic burden of implementation and reconstruction efforts will be determined by the compliance and active participation by all the authorities in Bosnia and Herzegovina in implementing the Peace Agreement and rebuilding a civil society, in particular in full cooperation with the International Tribunal for the Former Yugoslavia, in strengthening joint institutions and in facilitating returns of refugees and displaced persons;

3. Reminds the parties once again that, in accordance with the Peace Agreement, they have committed themselves to cooperate fully with all entities involved in the implementation of this peace settlement, as described in the Peace Agreement, or which are otherwise authorized by the Security Council, including the International Tribunal for the Former Yugoslavia, as it carries out its responsibilities for dispensing justice impartially, and underlines that full cooperation by States and entities with the International Tribunal includes, inter alia, the surrender for trial of all persons indicted by the Tribunal and provision of information to assist in Tribunal investigations;

4. Emphasizes its full support for the continued role of the High Representative in monitoring the implementation of the Peace Agreement and giving guidance to and coordinating the activities of the civilian organizations and agencies involved in assisting the parties to implement the Peace Agreement, and reaffirms that the High Representative is the final authority in theatre regarding the interpretation of Annex 10 on civilian implementation of the Peace Agreement and that in case of dispute he may give his interpretation and make recommendations, and make binding decisions as he judges necessary on issues as elaborated by the Peace Implementation Council in Bonn on 9 and 10 December 1997;

5. Expresses its support for the declaration of the Luxembourg Peace Implementation Council Steering Board;

6. Recognizes that the parties have authorized the multinational force referred to in paragraph 10 below to take such actions as required, including the use of necessary force, to ensure compliance with Annex 1–A of the Peace Agreement;

7. Reaffirms its intention to keep the situation in Bosnia and Herzegovina under close review, taking into account the reports submitted pursuant to paragraphs 18 and 25 below, and any recommendations those reports might include, and its readiness to consider the imposition of measures if any party fails significantly to meet its obligations under the Peace Agreement;

II

8. Pays tribute to those Member States who participated in the multinational stabilization force established in accordance with its resolution 1088 (1996) and welcomes their willingness to assist the parties to

the Peace Agreement by continuing to deploy a multinational stabilization force;

9. Notes the support of the parties to the Peace Agreement for the continuation of SFOR set out in the declaration of the Luxembourg
Peace Implementation Council Steering Board;

10. Authorizes the Member States acting through or in cooperation with
the organization referred to in Annex 1–A of the Peace Agreement to
continue for a further planned period of 12 months the multinational
stabilization force (SFOR) as established in accordance with its resolution 1088 (1996) under unified command and control in order to
fulfil the role specified in Annex 1–A and Annex 2 of the Peace Agreement and expresses its intention to review the situation with a view
to extending this authorization further as necessary in the light of developments in the implementation of the Peace Agreement and the situation in Bosnia and Herzegovina;

11. Authorizes the Member States acting under paragraph 10 above to
take all necessary measures to effect the implementation of and to ensure compliance with Annex 1–A of the Peace Agreement, stresses
that the parties shall continue to be held equally responsible for compliance with that Annex and shall be equally subject to such enforcement action by SFOR as may be necessary to ensure implementation
of that Annex and the protection of SFOR, and takes note that the
parties have consented to SFOR's taking such measures;

12. Authorizes Member States to take all necessary measures, at the request of SFOR, either in defence of SFOR or to assist the force in carrying out its mission, and recognizes the right of the force to take all
necessary measures to defend itself from attack or threat of attack;

13. Authorizes the Member States acting under paragraph 10 above, in
accordance with Annex 1–A of the Peace Agreement, to take all necessary measures to ensure compliance with the rules and procedures
established by the Commander of SFOR, governing command and
control of airspace over Bosnia and Herzegovina with respect to all
civilian and military air traffic;

14. Requests the authorities in Bosnia and Herzegovina to cooperate with
the Commander of SFOR to ensure the effective management of the
airports of Bosnia and Herzegovina, in the light of the responsibilities
conferred on SFOR by Annex 1–A of the Peace Agreement with regard to the airspace of Bosnia and Herzegovina;

15. Demands that the parties respect the security and freedom of movement of SFOR and other international personnel;

16. Invites all States, in particular those in the region, to continue to provide appropriate support and facilities, including transit facilities, for the Member States acting under paragraph 10 above;

17. Recalls all the agreements concerning the status of forces as referred to in Appendix B to Annex 1–A of the Peace Agreement, and reminds the parties of their obligation to continue to comply therewith;

18. Requests the member States acting through or in cooperation with the organization referred to in Annex 1–A of the Peace Agreement to continue to report to the Council, through the appropriate channels and at least at monthly intervals; Reaffirming the legal basis in the Charter of the United Nations on which the IPTF was given its mandate in resolution 1035 (1995),

III

19. Decides to extend the mandate of UNMIBH, which includes the IPTF, for an additional period terminating on 21 June 1999, and also decides that the IPTF shall continue to be entrusted with the tasks set out in Annex 11 of the Peace Agreement, including the tasks referred to in the Conclusions of–the London, Bonn and Luxembourg Conferences and agreed by the authorities in Bosnia and Herzegovina;

20. Requests the Secretary–General to keep the Council regularly informed on the work of the IPTF and its progress in assisting the restructuring of law enforcement agencies, and to report every three months on the implementation of the mandate of UNMIBH as a whole;

21. Reiterates that the successful implementation of the tasks of the IPTF rests on the quality, experience and professional skills of its personnel, and once again urges member States, with the support of the Secretary–General, to ensure the provision of such qualified personnel;

22. Reaffirms the responsibility of the parties to cooperate fully with, and instruct their respective responsible officials and authorities to provide their full support to, the IPTF on all relevant matters;

23. Reiterates its call upon all concerned to ensure the closest possible coordination between the High Representative, SFOR, UNMIBH and the relevant civilian organizations and agencies so as to ensure the successful implementation of the Peace Agreement and of the priority

objectives of the civilian consolidation plan, as well as the security of IPTF personnel;

24. Urges Member States, in response to demonstrable progress by the parties in restructuring their law enforcement institutions, to intensify their efforts to provide, on a voluntary–funded basis and in coordination with the IPTF, training, equipment and related assistance for local police forces in Bosnia and Herzegovina;

25. Also requests the Secretary–General to continue to submit to the Council reports from the High Representative, in accordance with Annex 10 of the Peace Agreement and the conclusions of the Peace Implementation Conference held in London on 4 and 5 December 1996 (S/1996/1012), on the implementation of the Peace Agreement and in particular on compliance by the parties with their commitments under that Agreement;

26. Decides to remain seized of the matter.

UNITED NATIONS SECURITY COUNCIL RESOLUTION 1186

Resolution 1186 (1998). Adopted By The Security Council At Its 3911th Meeting, On 21 July 1998 the Security Council,

Recalling all its previous relevant resolutions concerning the conflicts in the former Yugoslavia, in particular resolutions 1168 (1998) of 21 May 1998 and 1174 (1998) of 15 June 1998,

Recalling also the General Framework Agreement for Peace in Bosnia and Herzegovina and the Annexes thereto (collectively the Peace Agreement, S/1995/999, annex),

Taking note of the conclusions of the Peace Implementation Conference in Bonn on 9 and 10 December 1997 (S/1997/979, annex) and of the declaration of the Peace Implementation Council Steering Board in Luxembourg on 9 June 1998 (S/1998/498, annex),

Noting also the recommendations of the High Representative of 9 April 1998 (S/1998/314),

Having considered the reports of the Secretary–General of 12 March 1998 (S/1998/227 and Corr.1 and Add.1) and 10 June 1998 (S/1998/491), in particular his observations and planning regarding the issue of legal reform,

1. Approves the establishment by the United Nations Mission in Bosnia and Herzegovina (UNMIBH) of a programme to monitor and assess

the court system in Bosnia and Herzegovina, as part of an overall programme of legal reform as outlined by the office of the High Representative, in the light of the Peace Agreement, the recommendations
of the Peace Implementation Conference in Bonn and the Peace implementation Council Steering Board in Luxembourg, and the recommendations of the High Representative;

2. Requests the authorities in Bosnia and Herzegovina to cooperate fully
    with, and instruct their respective responsible officials to provide
    their full support to, the court monitoring programme;

3. Requests the Secretary–General to keep the Council. regularly in-
    formed on the implementation of the programme to monitor and as-
    sess the court system in Bosnia and Herzegovina through his reports
    on the implementation of the mandate of UNMIBH as a whole;

4. Decides to remain seized of the matter.

UNITED NATIONS SECURITY
COUNCIL RESOLUTION 1199

Adopted by the Security Council at its 3930th meeting, on 23 September
1998 the Security Council,
Recalling its resolution 1160 (1998) of 31 March 1998,
Having considered the reports of the Secretary–General pursuant to that
resolution, and in particular his report of 4 September 1998 (S/1998/834
and Add.1),
Noting with appreciation the statement of the Foreign Ministers of France,
Germany, Italy, the Russian Federation, the United Kingdom of Great Britain
and Northern Ireland and the United States of America (the Contact Group)
of 12 June 1998 at the conclusion of the Contact Group's meeting with the
Foreign Ministers of Canada and Japan (S/1998/567, annex), and the further
statement of the Contact Group made in Bonn on 8 July 1998 (S/1998/657),
Noting also with appreciation the joint statement by the Presidents of the
Russian Federation and the Federal Republic of Yugoslavia of 16 June 1998
(S/1998/526),
Noting further the communication by the Prosecutor of the International
Tribunal for the Former Yugoslavia to the Contact Group on 7 July 1998,
expressing the view that the situation in Kosovo represents an armed con-
flict within the terms of the mandate of the Tribunal,
Gravely concerned at the recent intense fighting in Kosovo and in particu-
lar the excessive and indiscriminate use of force by Serbian security forces

and the Yugoslav Army which have resulted in numerous civilian casualties and, according to the estimate of the Secretary–General, the displacement of over 230,000 persons from their homes,

Deeply concerned by the flow of refugees into northern Albania, Bosnia and Herzegovina and other European countries as a result of the use of force in Kosovo, as well as by the increasing numbers of displaced persons within Kosovo, and other parts of the Federal Republic of Yugoslavia, up to 50,000 of whom the United Nations High Commissioner for Refugees has estimated are without shelter and other basic necessities,

Reaffirming the right of all refugees and displaced persons to return to their homes in safety, and underlining the responsibility of the Federal Republic of Yugoslavia for creating the conditions which allow them to do so,

Condemning all acts of violence by any party, as well as terrorism in pursuit of political goals by any group or individual, and all external support for such activities in Kosovo, including the supply of arms and training for terrorist activities in Kosovo and expressing concern at the reports of continuing violations of the prohibitions imposed by resolution 1160 (1998),

Deeply concerned by the rapid deterioration in the humanitarian situation throughout Kosovo, alarmed at the impending humanitarian catastrophe as described in the report of the Secretary–General, and emphasizing the need to prevent this from happening,

Deeply concerned also by reports of increasing violations of human rights and of international humanitarian law, and emphasizing the need to ensure that the rights of all inhabitants of Kosovo are respected,

Reaffirming the objectives of resolution 1160 (1998), in which the Council expressed support for a peaceful resolution of the Kosovo problem which would include an enhanced status for Kosovo, a substantially greater degree of autonomy, and meaningful self–administration,

Reaffirming also the commitment of all Member States to the sovereignty and Territorial integrity of the Federal Republic of Yugoslavia,

Affirming that the deterioration of the situation in Kosovo, Federal Republic of Yugoslavia, constitutes a threat to peace and security in the region,

Acting under Chapter VII of the Charter of the United Nations,

1.   Demands that all parties, groups and individuals immediately cease hostilities and maintain a ceasefire in Kosovo, Federal Republic of Yugoslavia, which would enhance the prospects for a meaningful dialogue between the authorities of the Federal Republic of Yugoslavia and the Kosovo Albanian leadership and reduce the risks of a humanitarian catastrophe;

2. Demands also that the authorities of the Federal Republic of Yugoslavia and the Kosovo Albanian leadership take immediate steps to improve the humanitarian situation and to avert the impending humanitarian catastrophe;

3. Calls upon the authorities in the Federal Republic of Yugoslavia and the Kosovo Albanian leadership to enter immediately into a meaningful dialogue without preconditions and with international involvement, and to a clear timetable, leading to an end of the crisis and to a negotiated political solution to the issue of Kosovo, and welcomes the current efforts aimed at facilitating such a dialogue;

4. Demands further that the Federal Republic of Yugoslavia, in addition to the measures called for under resolution 1160 (1998), implement immediately the following concrete measures towards achieving a political solution to the situation in Kosovo as contained in the Contact Group statement of 12 June 1998: (a) cease all action by the security forces affecting the civilian population and order the withdrawal of security units used for civilian repression; (b) enable effective and continuous international monitoring in Kosovo by the European Community monitoring mission and diplomatic missions accredited to the Federal Republic of Yugoslavia, including access and complete freedom of movement of such monitors to, from and within Kosovo unimpeded by government authorities, and expeditious issuance of appropriate travel documents to international personnel contributing to the monitoring; (c) facilitate, in agreement with the UNHCR and the International Committee of the Red Cross (ICRC), the safe return of refugees and displaced persons to their homes and allow free and unimpeded access for humanitarian organizations and supplies to Kosovo; (d) make rapid progress to a clear timetable, in the dialogue referred to in paragraph 3 with the Kosovo Albanian community called for in resolution 1160 (1998), with the aim of agreeing confidence–building measures and finding a political solution to the problems of Kosovo;

5. Notes, in this connection, the commitments of the President of the Federal Republic of Yugoslavia, in his joint statement with the President of the Russian Federation of 16 June 1998: (a) to resolve existing problems by political means on the basis of equality for all citizens and ethnic communities in Kosovo; (b) not to carry out any repressive actions against the peaceful population; (c) to provide full freedom of movement for and ensure that there will be no reactions on representatives of foreign States and international institutions

accredited to the Federal Republic of Yugoslavia monitoring the situation in Kosovo; (d) to ensure full and unimpeded access for humanitarian organizations, the C and the UNHCR, and delivery of humanitarian supplies; (e) to facilitate the unimpeded return of refugees and displaced persons under programmes agreed with the UNHCR and the ICRC, providing State aid for the reconstruction of destroyed homes, and calls for the full implementation of these commitments;

6. Insists that the Kosovo Albanian leadership condemn all terrorist action, and emphasizes that all elements in the Kosovo Albanian community should pursue their goals by peaceful means only;

7. Recalls the obligations of all States to implement fully the prohibitions imposed by resolution 1160 (1998);

8. Endorses the steps taken to establish effective international monitoring of the situation in Kosovo, and in this connection welcomes the establishment of the Kosovo Diplomatic observer Mission;

9. Urges States and international organizations represented in the Federal Republic of Yugoslavia to make available personnel to fulfil the responsibility of carrying out effective and continuous international monitoring in Kosovo until the objectives of this resolution and those of resolution 1160 (1998) are achieved;

10. Reminds the Federal Republic of Yugoslavia that it has the primary responsibility for the security of all diplomatic personnel accredited to the Federal Republic of Yugoslavia as well as the safety and security of all international and non–governmental humanitarian personnel in the Federal Republic of Yugoslavia and calls upon the authorities of the Federal Republic of Yugoslavia and all others concerned in the Federal Republic of Yugoslavia to take all appropriate steps to ensure that monitoring personnel performing functions under this resolution are not subject to the threat or use of force or interference of any kind;

11. Requests States to pursue all means consistent with their domestic legislation and relevant international law to prevent funds collected on their territory being used to contravene resolution 1160 (1998);

12. Calls upon Member States and others concerned to provide adequate resources for humanitarian assistance in the region and to respond promptly and generously to the United Nations Consolidated Inter–Agency Appeal for Humanitarian Assistance Related to the Kosovo Crisis;

13. Calls upon the authorities of the Federal Republic of Yugoslavia, the leaders of the Kosovo Albanian community and all others concerned to cooperate fully with the Prosecutor of the International Tribunal for the Former Yugoslavia in the investigation of possible violations within the jurisdiction of the Tribunal;

14. Underlines also the need for the authorities of the Federal Republic of Yugoslavia to bring to justice those members of the security forces who have been involved in the mistreatment of civilians and the deliberate destruction of property;

15. Requests the Secretary–General to provide regular reports to the Council as necessary on his assessment of compliance with this resolution by the authorities of the Federal Republic of Yugoslavia and all elements in the Kosovo Albanian community, including through his regular reports on compliance with resolution 1160 (1998);

16. Decides, should the concrete measures demanded in this resolution and resolution 1160 (1998) not be taken, to consider further action and additional measures to maintain or restore peace and stability in the region;

17. Decides to remain seized of the matter.

NOTES

PREFACE

1. Raymond Tanter is professor of political science at the University of Michigan. He served on the National Security Council Staff at the White House. Tanter was personal representative of the secretary of defense to arms control talks in Helsinki, Madrid, and Stockholm—the Conference on Security and Cooperation in Europe—as well as to the Mutual and Balanced Force Reduction negotiations in Vienna.

   Dr. John Psarouthakis is distinguished professor of business administration at Eastern Michigan University and senior lecturer of mechanical engineering at the Massachusetts Institute of Technology. Psarouthakis was adjunct professor of business administration at the University of Michigan. He served as advisor to the prime minister of Greece. He is founder and former chief executive officer of JP Industries Inc., and JPE Inc., both manufacturers of durable goods for the automotive industry.

   Loretta Hieber, who conducted interviews for the book, served as producer and program coordinator with the Radio Partnership of the International Centre for Humanitarian Reporting based in Geneva and Cambridge, Massachusetts. She was an associate at the Michigan Journalism Fellows Program and an associate at the Harvard Program in Refugee Trauma.

2. When the text refers to "Bosnia," that term includes the Republic of Bosnia and Herzegovina, and "Serbia" includes the Federal Republic of Yugoslavia (Serbia and Montenegro). "Kosovo" is a southern province of Serbia, and resident ethnic Albanians are in conflict with

Serbia over independence or autonomy for Kosovo. Finally, "Republika Srpska" refers to Bosnian Serb controlled areas of the Republic of Bosnia and Herzegovina.

3. "During the Cold War, Greece and Turkey were in NATO, Bulgaria and Romania were in the Warsaw Pact, Yugoslavia was nonaligned, and Albania was an isolated sometime associate of communist China. Now these Cold War alignments are giving way to civilizational ones rooted in Islam and Orthodoxy. Balkan leaders talk of crystallizing a Greek–Serb–Bulgarian Orthodox alliance." Samuel Huntington, *The Clash of Civilizations and the Remaking of World Order* (New York: Simon and Schuster, 1996), 126–127.

4. Raymond Tanter and John Psarouthakis, "Next June is Too Soon for Troops to Abandon U.S. Mission in Bosnia," *Detroit Free Press,* 13 November 1997, sec. A, 19.

5. Richard Holbrooke, *To End a War* (New York: Random House, 1998); Warren Zimmermann, *Origins of a Catastrophe: Yugoslavia and Its Destroyers* (New York: Times Books, 1996); and Noel Malcolm, *Bosnia: A Short History* (New York: New York University Press, 1994).

6. Rebecca West, *Black Lamb and Grey Falcon* and Robert Kaplan, *Balkan Ghosts: A Journey through History* (New York: Vintage Books, 1993).

7. Benjamin Barber, "Jihad vs. McWorld," *The Atlantic Monthly,* (March 1992): 13. Also, see Benjamin Barber, *Jihad vs. McWorld* (New York: Ballantine Books, 1996).

8. "Lebanonization" and "Somalism" refer to disintegration of Lebanon and Somalia, respectively.

CHAPTER 1

1. "Clinton Returns Home from Bosnia after Encouraging Peace and Visiting U.S. Troops," New York Times on the Web, 22 December 1997. Available from: http://www.nytimes.com/97/12/22/late/

2. The American negotiating team, led by Richard Holbrooke, selected the Wright–Patterson Air Force Base in Dayton, Ohio, in order to hold talks among the parties to the Bosnian Conflict. See Richard

Holbrooke, *To End a War* (New York: Random House, 1998), 203–205.

3. Janice Stein, ed., *Getting to the Table: The Processes of International Prenegotiation* (Baltimore MD: The Johns Hopkins University Press, 1989), and Roger Fisher, *Getting to Yes: Negotiating Agreement without Giving In* (Boston: Houghton Mifflin, 1981).

4. Deterrence is a process of inducing a potential challenger not to take an action; coercive diplomacy aims at getting an actor to take an action or undo something already in place. Coercive diplomacy combines the threat of force and economic sanctions with diplomacy. See Alexander George and Richard Smoke, *Deterrence in American Foreign Policy* (New York: Columbia University Press, 1974); and Alexander George, David Hall, and William Simons, *The Limits of Coercive Diplomacy* (Boston: Little Brown, 1971).

5. One approach within the field of cognitive psychology is prospect theory. See Daniel Kahneman and Amos Tversky, "Prospect Theory: An Analysis of Decision under Risk," Econometrica 47 (1979): 263. For an application in political science, see Jack Levy, "An Introduction to Prospect Theory," in Barbara Farnham, ed., *Avoiding Losses/Taking Risks: Prospect Theory and International Conflict* (Ann Arbor: University of Michigan Press, 1994), 7–22.

6. United Nations, International Tribunal for the Prosecution of Persons Responsible for Serious Violations of International Humanitarian Law Committed in the Territory of Former Yugoslavia since 1991 in The Hague, Netherlands. Available from: http://www.un.org/icty/970507jt.htm

7. Illustrative of the literature on the balance of power are: Inis Claude, *Swords into Plowshares: The Problems and Progress of International Organization*, 2d ed. (New York: Random House, 1959); Henry Kissinger, *A World Restored: Metternich, Castlereagh and the Problems of Peace, 1812–22,* (Boston: Houghton Mifflin, 1957).

8. A. F. K. Organski, *World Politics,* 2d ed. (New York: Knopf, 1968); Bruce Bueno de Mesquita, *The War Trap* (New Haven, CT: Yale University Press, 1981); Paul Huth and Bruce Russett, "What Makes Deterrence Work? Cases from 1900 to 1980," *World Politics* 36, no. 4 (July 1984), 496–526.

Robert Pape provides a succinct statement of the role that pre-ponderance of power plays in coercion: "Striking military targets in the adversary's homeland shifts the military balance, thereby compelling the victim to modify its behavior." Robert Pape, *Bombing to Win: Air Power and Coercion in War* (Ithaca, NY: Cornell University Press, 1996), 5.

9. Ze'ev Maoz, "Resolve, Capability, and the Outcomes of Interstate Disputes, 1816–1976," *Journal of Conflict Resolution* 27, no. 2 (June 1983), 195–229; Dina A. Zinnes, Robert C. North, and Howard E. Koch Jr., "Capability, Threat, and the Outbreak of War," *International Politics and Foreign Policy,* James N. Rosenau ed., (New York: Free Press, 1961), 469–482.

10. Thomas Schelling, *Arms and Influence* (New Haven CT: Yale University Press, 1966). Also see, Ze'ev Maoz, "Resolve, Capability, and the Outcomes of Interstate Disputes, 1816–1976," *Journal of Conflict Resolution* 27, no. 2 (June 1983), 195–229. Maoz holds that, "the willingness and ability to expose the civilian population to enemy strikes is an indicator of resolve. So is, however, the willingness to inflict punishment on civilians. The two are connected because once you decide to attack the opponent's population, you run a higher risk of getting your own civilians hit," from an electronic mail message to Raymond Tanter, June 24, 1998, the Baker Institute of Public Policy Rice University, Houston, TX. In a related vein, Steve Rosen discusses "cost–tolerance," which may be interpreted as a willingness of a regime to expose its population to harm, that is, the degree of that regime's resolve. See Steve Rosen, "War Power and the Willingness to Suffer," in Bruce Russett, ed., *War, Peace, and Numbers* (Beverly Hills, CA: Sage, 1972), 167–183.

11. Noel Malcolm, *Kosovo a Short History* (New York: New York University Press, 1998), chapter 1. Also see, Anna Husarska, "Blood Feud," *New York Times* (August 9, 1998). A book review of Noel Malcolm, *Kosovo a Short History* and Miranda Vickers, *Between Serb and Albanian a History of Kosovo* (New York: Columbia University Press, 1998).

12. Jack Snyder, "Saving Face for the Sake of Deterrence," in Robert Jervis, Richard Ned Lebow, and Janice Gross Stein, eds., *Psychology and Deterrence* (Baltimore, MD: The Johns Hopkins University Press,

1985), 155. For an elaboration for the offense/defense nexus, see Robert Harkavy, *Preemption and Two–Front Conventional Warfare* (Jerusalem: Leonard Davis Institute for International Relations, Hebrew University of Jerusalem, Papers on Peace Problems, 1977), 8. Harkavy distinguishes between preemptive attack and preventive war. In preemption, the threatened actor places a premium on offensive action, but in prevention, that actor does not perceive striking the first blow as crucial. In a decision to launch a preventive war, "What *is* important is the forestalling of a change in the balance of power;" Robert Harkavy, *Preemption and Two–Front Conventional Warfare,* 7 [emphasis in original].

13. See Ned Lebow, "Window of Opportunity" and Robert Jervis, "Introduction," in Robert Jervis, Ned Lebow, and Janice Gross Stein, *Psychology and Deterrence,* 147–86, 1–12.

CHAPTER 2

1. "Serbia and Montenegro have asserted the formation of a joint independent state, but this entity has not been formally recognized as a state by the United States; the U.S. view is that the Socialist Federal Republic of Yugoslavia (SFRY) has dissolved and that none of the successor republics represents its continuation." *Central Intelligence Agency World Factbook, 1997.* Available from: http://www.odci.gov/cia/publications/factbook/country-frame.html

2. Susan Woodward, *Balkan Tragedy: Chaos and Dissolution after the Cold War* (Washington D.C.: The Brookings Institution, 1995), 90, endnote omitted.

3. "After the speech of June 28, 1989, Milosevic ... acquired an unchallengeable personal standing in Serbia, by a combination of Communist methods and nationalist rhetoric." Noel Malcolm, *Bosnia: A Short History* (New York: New York University Press, 1996), 213.

4. Warren Zimmermann, *Origins of a Catastrophe: Yugoslavia and Its Destroyers* (New York: Times Books, 1996) 132.
   Ambassador Zimmermann is a proponent of the first school of thought in this book, that is, politicians manipulate ethnic tensions for their own political gains. In this respect, Zimmermann held that

Milosevic used Serbian nationalism as an opportunity to come to power in Yugoslavia. Zimmermann, *Origins of a Catastrophe*, 234.

5. For a discussion of biases and perception, see Daniel Kahneman, Paul Slovic, and Amos Tversky, *Judgment under Uncertainty: Heuristics and Biases* (New York : Cambridge University Press, 1982).

6. Richard Holbrooke, *To End a War* (New York: Random House, 1998), 27; and James Baker A. III, *The Politics of Diplomacy* (New York: G.P. Putnam's Sons, 1995), 483, 635.

7. Interview by Loretta Hieber with Mate Granic, minister of foreign affairs, government of Croatia, July 3, 1996, Zagreb.

8. See Chapter Five: "Conflict: Circumstance and Choice" for a further explication of these two concepts.

9. Samuel Huntington, *The Clash of Civilizations and Remaking the World Order* (New York: Simon and Schuster, 1996) 127.

10. For a critique of balance-of-power principles such as "The enemy of my enemy is my friend," see Bruce Jentleson, *With Friends Like These: Reagan, Bush, and Saddam, 1982–1990* (New York: W.W. Norton, 1994), 15 ff.

11. For a further explication of the Iranian connection in arms transshipments to Bosnia, see Kristin McLean "Washington's Green Light to Tehran for Arms to Sarajevo via Zagreb?" Unpublished paper prepared for the course Political Science 472 at the University of Michigan, (Spring 1996). Available from: http://www–personal.umich.edu/~rtanter/S96PS472_Papers

This endnote appears in Raymond Tanter, *Rogue Regimes: Terrorism and Proliferation* (New York: St. Martin's Press, 1998), 72.

12. Interview by Loretta Hieber with Lord David Owen, chief European Union negotiator for Yugoslavia, July 29, 1996, London. Also see David Owen, *Balkan Odyssey* (New York: Harcourt Brace, 1995).

13. For a discussion of the Brioni Accord, see *World Statesman: Politics and Current Affairs Magazine*, Kensington Publications 1996, fourth quarter 1996. Available from: http://www.kenpubs.co.uk/worldstatesman/Archive/Kucan.html

14. The population of Slovenia at the 1991 census was almost 2 million. A Slavic ethnic group, the Slovenes, account for roughly 90 percent of the republic's population. Ethnic Serbs make up about 2 percent of

the population. But by the early 1990s, there were about 60,000 refugees from the Bosnian War in Slovenia.

15. During 1991, the population of Croatia was about 4.8 million. Ethnically, Croats were about 78 percent of that country's population. Within Croatia, the largest minority is of Serb origin. Many of the Serbs lived in the Serb–held enclaves of Krajina (in western and central Croatia) and eastern Slavonia (in northeastern Croatia). Other Serbs resided in Zagreb. Other ethnic groups in Croatia include a Muslim population of less than 1 percent.

CHAPTER 3

1. Interview by Loretta Hieber with Pauline Neville–Jones, former British head political officer of the foreign ministry, July 29, 1996, London. Jones was an architect of the Contact Group, comprised of Britain, France, Germany, the United States, and the Soviet Union.

2. Interview by Loretta Hieber with Christian Reuilly, head of the Bosnian policy desk at the French Foreign Ministry, June 24, 1996, Paris.

3. Interview by Loretta Hieber with Hans Ulrich–Seidt, Yugoslav desk of the German Foreign Office, June 11, 1996, Bonn.

4. Johann Georg Reismuller said that Germany, " . . . should be particularly sensitive to the fact that a nearby country (Serbia) is possessed with the same madness [that the Nazis had, "ubermensch"], and is harassing weaker ones, Slovenia and Croatia." Johann Georg Reismuller, *Frankfurter Allgemeine Zeitung,* February 26, 1991.

5. Interview by Loretta Hieber with Hans Ulrich–Seidt, Yugoslav desk of the German Foreign Office, June 11, 1996, Bonn.

6. Interview by Loretta Hieber with Alain Charleton, British Foreign Office, July 29, 1996, London and with Gojko Susak, minister of defense, government of Croatia, July 6, 1996, Zagreb.

7. Bosnia's population of over three million in the early 1990s has an ethnic composition of about 40 percent Serbian, 38 percent Muslim, and 22 percent Croat.

8. Interview by Loretta Hieber with Mirza Hajric, government of Bosnia adviser for international relations and foreign affairs, July 4, 1996.

9. For an analysis of war termination conditions, see Fred Ikle, *Every War Must End* (New York: Columbia University Press, 1991).

10. Art Pines, "Bush Warns Serbia against Escalation," *Los Angeles Times,* 29 December 1992, sec. A, 4.

11. David Owen, *Balkan Odyssey* (New York: Harcourt Brace, 1995), 89–150.

12. Interview by Loretta Hieber with Mate Granic, minister of foreign affairs, government of Croatia, July 3, 1996, Zagreb.

13. Interview by Loretta Hieber with Lord David Owen, chief European Union negotiator for Yugoslavia, July 29, 1996, London.

14. Interview by Loretta Hieber with Mirza Hajric, government of Bosnia adviser for international relations and foreign affairs, July 4, 1996.

15. Interview by Loretta Hieber with Mate Granic, minister of foreign affairs, government of Croatia, July 3, 1996, Zagreb.

16. Interview by Loretta Hieber with Lord David Owen, chief European Union negotiator for Yugoslavia, July 29, 1996, London.

17. Interview by Loretta Hieber with Alain Charleton, British Foreign Office, July 29, 1996, London.

18. Interview by Loretta Hieber with Mirza Hajric, government of Bosnia adviser for international relations and foreign affairs, July 4, 1996.

19. Interview by Loretta Hieber with Alain Charleton, British Foreign Office, July 29, 1996, London.

20. Interview by Loretta Hieber with General Phillipe Morillon, former United Nations commander in Bosnia, June 24, 1996, Paris.

21. Interview by Loretta Hieber with Alain Charleton, British Foreign Office, July 29, 1996, London.

22. Interview by Loretta Hieber with Pauline Neville–Jones, former British head political officer of the foreign ministry, July 29, 1996.

23. Interview by Loretta Hieber with Gojko Susak, minister of defense, government of Croatia, July 6, 1996, Zagreb.

24. Interview by Loretta Hieber with Hido Biscevic, senior policy analyst for the ministry of foreign affairs of Croatia, July 6, 1996, Zagreb.

25. Interview by Loretta Hieber with Mate Granic, minister of foreign affairs, government of Croatia, July 3, 1996, Zagreb.

26. Interview by Loretta Hieber with Alain Charleton, British Foreign Office, July 29, 1996, London.

27. For a study of the coercive effect of airpower, see Robert Pape, *Bombing to Win: Air Power and Coercion in War* (Ithaca, NY: Cornell University Press, 1996). Also see Lt. Col. Peter Faber, U.S. Air Force, "Competing Theories of Airpower: A Language for Analysis," Derived from the temporary site http://www.cdsar.af.mil/presentation/faber.html

28. See NATO gopher "Operation Deny Flight." IFOR Operation Deny Flight Final Factsheet, December 21, 1995. Available from: http://www.nato.int/ifor/general/fs–fin.htm

29. For a further discussion of Deny Flight, see Chapter Four: "Coercive Diplomacy."

30. The term Bosnia includes the entity Bosnia–Herzegovina, and the term Serbia consists of Serbia–Montenegro.

31. Fedarko, Kevin. "The Guns of August," *Time,* August 14, 1995, 44–45, Knight, Robin. "Risking Wider War," *U.S. News & World Report,* August 14, 1995, 28–29.

32. "As the Bosnian case demonstrates, unless pressure is exerted on both sides to moderate their demands, intervention will not necessarily enhance the prospects for agreement . . . the United States did place pressure on all the combatants and brought the parties to an agreement in Dayton."

    David Lake (University of California, San Diego) and Donald Rothchild, (University of California, Davis), "Ethnic Fears and Global Engagement: The International Spread and Management of Global Conflict," Commissioned paper for the IGCC Working Group Conference on the International Spread and Management of Ethnic Conflict, October 1, 1994, 75.

33. David Owen, *Balkan Odyssey* (London: V. Gollancz, 1995).

34. "Bosnia's Glimmer of Peace." *The Economist,* January 23, 1993, 45–46. "They Call It Peace," *The Economist,* August 28, 1993, 44–46. "Another Map for Bosnia," *The Economist,* July 9, 1994, 47. "A Perilous Peace," *Time,* December 4, 1995, 30–35.

35. The Dayton Proximity Talks culminated in the initialing of a General Framework Agreement for Peace in Bosnia and Herzegovina by the Republic of Bosnia and Herzegovina, the Republic of Croatia and the Federal Republic of Yugoslavia (Serbia–Montenegro). The European Union special negotiator and representatives of the Contact Group

nations—the United States, Britain, France, Germany, and Russia—witnessed the initialing. Summary of the General Framework Agreement, Fact Sheet Released by the Office of the Spokesman, U.S. Department of State, November 30, 1995. Available from: http://www.nato.int/ifor/gfa/gfa-summ.htm

36. United States Information Agency European Branch, "Public Opinion in Bosnia Herzegovina: One Year of Peace," (Washington, DC: Office of Research and Media Reaction, vol. 4, February 1997), 36. USIA, "Public Opinion," February 1997, Table 43, p. 50.

37. For an illustration of the accommodation to ethnic separateness in Dayton, see Article I: Inter–Entity Boundary Line.

38. Articles 1 and 2 of Annex 4 in the Dayton Peace Agreement mandated that Bosnia and Herzegovina consist of the two Entities, the Federation of Bosnia and Herzegovina and the Republika Srpska (hereinafter "the Entities"). Annex 4 called for the freedom of movement throughout Bosnia and Herzegovina. In addition, Article 1 stipulated that: (a) All citizens of either Entity are thereby citizens of Bosnia and Herzegovina. (b) No person shall be deprived of Bosnia and Herzegovina or Entity citizenship on any ground such as sex, race, color, language, religion, political or other opinion, national or social origin, association with a national minority, property, birth or other status.

39. Before Dayton, the Army of Republika Srpska (VRS) controlled some 45 percent of the territory of Bosnia– Herzegovina in late 1995. Just under 1.7 million people had lived in these areas before the war: 33 percent of them Bosniaks, 12 percent Croats, and 7 percent Yugoslavs or others, along with 48 percent Serbs. Post-Dayton territorial transfers have led to an entirely different ethnic profile in the Republika Srpska: just 3 percent Bosniaks, 1 percent Croats, and 7 percent Yugoslavs or others, along with the 89 percent Serbs. Praso, Murat, "Demographic Consequences of the 1992–1995 War," *Most ['Bridge']*, Mostar, No. 93, March–April 1996. Also available from: Bosnia Report http://www.barnsdle.demon.co.uk/bosnia/dem.html

40. Dayton Peace Agreement, Annex 4: "Each Entity shall provide all necessary assistance to the government of Bosnia and Herzegovina in order to enable it to honor the international obligations of Bosnia and Herzegovina, provided that financial obligations incurred by one En-

tity without the consent of the other prior to the election of the Parliamentary Assembly and Presidency of Bosnia and Herzegovina shall be the responsibility of that Entity, except insofar as the obligation is necessary for continuing the membership of Bosnia and Herzegovina in an international organization." Annex 9: "The Parties hereby establish a Commission on Public Corporations (the "Commission") to examine establishing Bosnia and Herzegovina Public Corporations to operate joint public facilities, such as for the operation of utility, energy, postal and communication facilities, for the benefit of both Entities." See the Appendix for a full statement of the Dayton Accords.

41. Gojko Klickovic, Prime Minister of Republika Srpska, personal interview by Vanja Bulic, June 1995, Belgrade Serbia. Derived from the temporary site http://wnc.fedworld.gov/cgibin/re.22ysp&CID=C280 7312011718757861073

42. United States Information Agency, "Bosnian Serbs, Croats, and Muslims Grow Further Apart in 'Vision' for Country," *Opinion Analysis,* (Washington, DC: Office of Research and Media Reaction, August 13, 1996) USIA, "Public Opinion," February 1997, table 35, 43.

43. For the 1996 poll, see United States Information Agency, "Bosnian Serb Opinion at Odds with Creating Multiethnic Society" *Opinion Analysis,* (Washington, DC: Office of Research and Media Reaction, August 12, 1996). USIA, "Basic Tenets of Multiethnic Society Endorsed By Relatively Few Bosnian Croats," *Opinion Analysis,* (Washington, DC: Office of Research and Media Reaction, April 25, 1996). USIA, "Bosnian Muslims Emphasize Own Ethnic Group Interests in Broad Acceptance of Ideals for Multiethnic Society," *Opinion Analysis,* (Washington, DC: Office of Research and Media Reaction, May 13, 1996). For the 1997 poll, see United States Information Agency European Branch, "Public Opinion in Bosnia Herzegovina: One Year of Peace," (Washington, DC: Office of Research and Media Reaction, vol. 4, February 1997), table 158, 164.

44. This description of ethnic conflicts and interventionist solutions draws on an discussion of the role of outsiders in ethnic conflicts by Timothy Sisk, *Power Sharing and International Mediation in Ethnic Conflicts* (Washington: United States Institute of Peace and the Carnegie Commission on Preventing Deadly Conflict, June 1996). Available from: http://www.carnegie.org/deadly/sisk.html

CHAPTER 4

1. Alexander George, *Forceful Persuasion: Coercive Diplomacy as an Alternative to War* (Washington, D.C.: United States Institute of Peace Press, 1991), 4–7.

2. Elliot Aronson, Timothy Wilson, and Robin Akert, *Social Psychology: The Heart and the Mind* (New York: Harper Collins, 1994).

3. Graham Allison, Albert Carnesale, and Joseph Nye, *Hawks, Doves, and Owls* (New York: W. W. Norton, 1985), 206–22. In addition to these three, others scholars have used the hawk–dove framework. See also Fred Ikle, *Every War Must End* (New York: Columbia University Press, 1991), 60–61, for his analysis of hawks and doves. Ikle defines hawks as those who engage in treasonous adventurism instead of terminating the fighting: in search of peace with honor, they fight too much and for too long. Doves are those who give aid and comfort to the enemy by retreating in the face of aggression: in a quest for peace at any cost, they would fight too little and for too short a time.

4. For a description of the bureaucratic state of play on Bosnia, see Ivo Daalder, *Anthony Lake and the War in Bosnia,* Pew Case Study number 467, 1995.

5. See UN Security Council Resolution 757, May 30, 1992, available from: gopher://gopher.undp.org:70/00/undocs/scd/scouncil/s92/32 or: http://www.nato.int/ifor/un/u920530a.htm

   In this book, actions by the United Nations and United States toward Serbia apply to Montenegro as well. Similarly, references to Bosnia apply to Herzegovina.

6. Office of Foreign Assets Control, "A summary involving the Federal Republic of Yugoslavia (Serbia and Montenegro) (including Executive Order 13088 relating to Kosovo)," Washington, DC: Department of the Treasury, June 18, 1998.

   On October 25, 1994, the United States imposed additional measures to target Bosnian Serb–controlled areas of the Republic of Bosnia and Herzegovina, the so called the Republika Srpska. Washington suspended the sanctions regarding prospective transactions in early 1996. But assets blocked prior to December 27, 1995 remain blocked in June 1998. With respect to the Serbian crackdown on ethnic Albanians in the Kosovo region of Serbia, President Clinton issued Executive Order 13088 on June 9, 1998, imposing new sanctions on Serbia.

7. UN Security Council Resolution 816 is available from: gopher://gopher.undp.org:70/00/undocs/scd/scouncil/s93/17

8. NATO press release, April 12, 1993, "NATO Starts Operation of No-Fly Zone Enforcement," available from: gopher://gopher.nato.int:70/00/natodata/PRESS/NATOPRESS/PRESS-93/pr29.93

9. UN Security Council Resolution 836, available from: gopher://gopher.undp.org:70/00/undocs/scd/scouncil/s93/37

10. Steven Erlanger, "Has the West Learned From Mistakes in Bosnia?" *New York Times,* June 10, 1998.

11. Art Pines, "Bush Warns Serbia against Escalation," *Los Angeles Times,* December 29, 1992, sec. A, 4.

12. Richard Holbrooke, *To End a War* (New York: Random House, 1998), 357.

13. R. Jeffrey Smith, "U.S. Envoy Warns Serbs, Kosovo Rebels," *Washington Post,* March 11, 1998, sec. A, 21. Also see: U.S. Senate, Committee on Armed Services, Statement by Robert Gelbard, Special Representative of the President and the Secretary of State for Implementation of the Dayton Peace Accords, June 4, 1998. Washington DC. Available from: http://www.state.gov/www/policy_remarks/1998/980604_gelbard_bosnia1.html

14. Steven Erlanger, "U.S. Says It Will Support NATO Strike in Kosovo," *New York Times,* June 9, 1998.

15. UN Security Council Resolution 1199, September 23, 1998. Available from: http://www.state.gov/www/regions/eur/rpt_981013_serbcomp.html

16. CNN Interactive, "Holbrooke, Milosevic Talk Again: U.S. B-52s moved to Europe as NATO Decision on Kosovo Looms," October 11, 1998. Available from: http://www.cnn.com/WORLD/europe/9810/11/kosovo.02/

17. Charles Krauthammer, "We Don't Need to Inflict," *Washington Post,* February 26, 1999, A27.

18. Robert Kaplan, "Why the Balkans Demand Amorality," *Washington Post,* February 28, 1999, B01.

19. Secretary of State Madeleine K. Albright, Press Conference on Kosovo, Brussels, Belgium, October 8, 1998. Available from: http://secretary.state.gov/www/statements/1998/981008.html

CHAPTER 5

1. One former policymaker contends that " . . . the concept of ethnic hatred served to obscure understanding of the war [in Bosnia] and to
justify inaction by the leadership." Wayne Bert, *The Reluctant Super-
power: United States' Policy in Bosnia, 1991–1995* (New York: St.
Martin's Press, 1997), 106.

2. For a discussion of the relationship between rationality, losses, and
gains see Daniel Kahneman and Amos Tversky, "Prospect Theory: An
Analysis of Decision Under Risk," *Econometrica* 47 (1979): 263.

   For an application of prospect theory to political decisionmaking, see Barbara Farnham, ed. *Avoiding Losses/Taking Risks:
Prospect Theory and International Conflict,* (Ann Arbor: University
of Michigan Press, 1994).

3. United States Information Agency, "Support for Multi Ethnic Society
is Limited Among Bosnian Public," European Opinion Alert, (Washington, DC: Office of Research and Media Reaction, June 26, 1996).

4. Coalition for International Justice. Available from: http://www.
wcw.org/wcw/icty/suspects.html

5. See the following source submitted by the Center for Security Policy,
"Thanks, but No Thanks: Clinton Should Back Bosnia in Rejecting
Vance–Owen 'Peace in Our Time,'" Decision Brief, February 4, 1993.
It is a source of the Vance–Owen peace plan, its major flaws, and
steps President Clinton should take. Derived from the temporary site
http://www.security–policy.org/papers/93–D13.html

6. For a summary of the Bosnian Serb reaction to the proposed
Vance–Owen peace plan, see "An Early Hope for Peace," Derived
from the temporary site: http://www.iinet.net.au/~digicom/
balkan.htm

7. As recorded by the United States Army, the Bosnian Serbs over-
whelmingly rejected the Vance–Owen peace plan in the 1993 referendum. Dr. Timothy L. Sanz, United States Army, "The Yugoslav
Conflict: a Chronology of Events 1990–1993," (Foreign Military
Studies Office, Fort Leavenworth, KS, November 1996). Available
from: http://www–leav.army.mil/fmso/geo/pubs/chronmr.htm

8. During the 1991 election campaign Dr. Franjo Tudjman stated that
he was grateful that his wife was neither a Serb nor a Jew. Ivancic,

Viktor, "Race and Power," *Feral Tribune,* Split, Croatia, June 3, 1996. Available from: http://www.cdsp.neu.edu/info/students/marko/feral/feral32.html

A hate article written by a Croatian on the Internet illustrates the effect ethnic outbidding has had on followers of the ethnic elites. "Death to Chetniks!" article submitted by Croboy on January 30, 1997. Available from: http://geog.gmu.edu/gess/jwc/bosnia/feedback/DEATHTOCHETNIKS.html

9.   For a discussion of the effect of motivated and unmotivated biases on perception, see Robert Jervis, "Perceiving and Coping with Threat," Robert Jervis, Ned Lebow, and Janice Gross Stein, eds., *Psychology and Deterrence,* (Baltimore, MD: The Johns Hopkins University Press, 1985), 18–27.

10. Preston Mendenhall, "Strong Ultimatum sent to Belgrade," *MSNBC,* June 12, 1998.

11. Bette Denich, "Unmaking Multi–Ethnicity in Yugoslavia: Metamorphosis Observed," *Anthropology of East Europe Review,* vol. 11, Nos. 1–2, 48.

12. Boris Dezulovic, "The Great Mover," *Feral Tribune,* (Split, Croatia, September 11, 1995).

13. Interview of James Harff, director of Ruder & Finn Global Public Affairs (a public relations company), personal interview by Jacques Merlino, October 1993, Paris, France.

14. For an excellent analysis of how symbolic politics was used in the former Yugoslavia to mobilize ethnic support, see Robert M. Hayden, "Recounting the Dead: The Rediscovery and Redefinition of Wartime Massacres in Late- and Post-Communist Yugoslavia," 167–184.

CHAPTER 6

1.   Mike O'Connor, *New York Times,* "G.I. Disinterest is a Casualty in Bosnia," January 4, 1998, sec. A, 6.

2.   Christine I. Wallich and Barbara S. Balaj, "Multilateralism and Post-Conflict Reconstruction: Bosnia–Herzegovina and the West Bank and Gaza," unpublished paper, 1998.

3.   Wallich and Balaj, "Multilateralism and Post-Conflict Reconstruction."

4. Robert Axelrod, *The Evolution of Cooperation* (New York: Basic Books, 1984).

5. Mancur Olson, Jr. "A Theory of Groups and Organizations," Bruce Russett, ed., *Economic Theories of International Politics* (Chicago: Markham, 1968), 143, 139–144. The pages in the Olson book are from 44–52.

6. Judith Ingram, "Biggest Fair of Stolen Cars Seen as Beacon of Harmony," *Detroit Free Press,* October 22, 1997.

7. Chris Hedges, "At Last, a Unifying Force in Bosnia: Making Money," *New York Times,* 17 October 1996, sec. A, 4.

    "The ethnic hatred all share is put aside in the interests of need and economic gain." "Once people's sense of national identity is secured, the appeal of radical nationalist politicians will evaporate and a reasonable politics and economics can emerge." Charles Boyd, "Making Bosnia Work," 52.

8. USIA, "Public Opinion," February 1997, tables 136–138, 146–147.

    One focus group member in Banja Luka recognized that "Money and business do not recognize borders." USIA, "Public Opinion," February 1997, 140.

9. "Peace Plan Provides Basis, Fuel Brings Enemies Back Together," (c) copyright 1996 Nando.net, Associated Press, KISELJAK, Bosnia–Herzegovina. Available from: http://www.nando.net/newsroom/nt/0128yugiii.html

10. Personal interview of Mr. Besniak by Loretta Hieber, July 3, 1996, Zagreb, Croatia.

11. Annex 10: Civilian Implementation, Dayton Peace Agreement, U.S. Department of State, Summary of the Dayton Peace Agreement on Bosnia–Herzegovina, Fact Sheet Released by the Office of the Spokesman, November 30, 1995. Available from: http://www.state.gov/www/regions/eur/bosnia/bossumm.html

    But the beautiful phrases of the Dayton Peace Agreement would amount to little more than a cruel fiction if, " . . . the powerful nations of the world were not prepared to add flesh to them—to exercise their will and make them real." Mark Danner, "Clinton, the UN, and the Bosnian Disaster," *The New York Review,* vol. XLIV, no. 20, December 18, 1997, 65–81. Also see "The US and the Yugoslav Catastrophe," *The New York Review,* vol. XLIV, no. 19, December 4, 1997, 55–65.

12. Carolyn Compton, civil affairs specialist, Army Reserve Unit, Kala-
    mazoo, Michigan, telephone interview by Elena Thomas, September
    17, 1997, Ann Arbor, Michigan.
        U.S. assistance programs provide such aid as food, clothing, the re-
    pairing of homes, hospitals, gas lines, and heating systems. These pro-
    grams are moving from providing humanitarian aid to ultimately
    reconstructing the Bosnian economy by rehabilitating the infrastructure
    and revitalizing commercial interactions. See, "Implementing the Day-
    ton Peace accords: The Role of the U.S. in Civil Implementation," Bu-
    reau of Public Affairs, 5 March 1996. Derived from the temporary site:
    http://www.state.gov/www/regions/eur/bosnia/bosnia_us_role.html
13. Charles Boyd, "Making Bosnia Work," *Foreign Affairs,* (vol. 77, no.
    1, January/February 1998), 42–55.
14. Charles Boyd, "Making Bosnia Work," 47.

CHAPTER 7

1. John Mearsheimer, "A Peace Agreement that's Bound to Fail," *New
   York Times,* October 19, 1998, Op. ed. page.
2. Graham Fuller and Ian Lesser, *A Sense of Siege: The Geopolitics of
   Islam and the West* (Boulder, CO, Westview Press, 1995), 54.
3. Samuel Huntington, *The Clash of Civilizations and the Remaking of
   World Order,* (New York: Simon and Schuster, 1996), 157–160.
4. Robert Kaplan, "Why the Balkans Demand Amorality," *Washington
   Post,* February 28, 1999, B01. Also see Robert Kaplan, *Balkan
   Ghosts: A Journey through History* (New York: Vintage Books,
   1994).
5. The United States government officially calls Macedonia the former
   Yugoslav Republic of Macedonia, which is the provisional name
   under which the country was admitted to the United Nations. Washington probably will continue to do so as long as the United Nations
   is mediating talks on the differences between the former Yugoslav Republic of Macedonia and Greece.
6. Vernon Loeb, "A Global, Pan-Islamic Network Terrorism Entrepreneur Unifies Groups Financially, Politically" *Washington Post,* August 23, 1998, sec. A, 1.

7.   R. Jeffrey Smith, "Albania Expands Crackdown on Arabs," *Washington Post,* August 29, 1998, sec. A, 10.

8.   James Risen, "Administration Defends Bosnian Arms Policy," *Los Angeles Times,* April 24, 1996, sec. A.

9.   United States Information Agency, "Support for Multi Ethnic Society is Limited Among Bosnian Public," European Opinion Alert, (Washington, DC: Office of Research and Media Reaction, June 26, 1996). United States Information Agency, "Bosnian Serbs, Croats and Muslims Grow Further Apart in 'Vision' for Country," Opinion Analysis, (Washington, DC: Office of Research and Media Reaction, August 13, 1996).

10. The Dayton Peace Agreement, Annex 2, contains an agreement on the boundaries of the Federation of Bosnia and the Serb Republic within Bosnia.

11. Susan Woodward, "America's Bosnia Policy: The Work Ahead," (Washington, DC: Brookings Policy Brief No. 2, May 1996). Available from: http://www.brook.edu/FP/POLBRIEF/Polbrf2.htm

12. Robert Schaeffer, *Warpaths: The Politics of Partition* (New York: Hill and Wang, 1990), 154–156.

13. United States Information Agency, "Many Refugees Choose Not to Return to Areas Controlled by New Government," *Opinion Analysis,* (Washington, DC: Office of Research and Media Reaction, June 3, 1996).

14. United Nations High Commission for Refugees report March 1997 (The World, Europe, Bosnia-Hercegovina) Available from: http://www.unhcr.ch/world/euro/bosnia.htm

15. Steven Erlanger," The Dayton Peace Agreement: A Status Report," *New York Times,* June 10, 1996. Available from: http://www.nytimes.com/specials/bosnia/context/dayton.html

     In addition, the Central Intelligence Agency 1996 World Factbook provides the following estimates for population size: Bosnia, 2,656,240; Croatia, 5,004,112; and Serbia, 10,614,558. Derived from the temporary site http://www.odci.gov/cia/publications/nsolo/factbook/eur.htm#S

16. Central Intelligence Agency, *World Factbook 1996: Bosnia.* Derived from the temporary site http://www.odci.gov/cia/publications/nsolo/factbook/bk.htm#Economy CEEBIC Site, Southeastern Europe Busi-

ness Brief, vol. 2.8, February 26, 1997. Derived from the temporary site http://www.iep.doc/eebic/ceebic.html

17. Schaeffer, *Warpaths: The Politics of Partition,* 159.
18. Schaeffer, *Warpaths: The Politics of Partition,* 255.
19. Schaeffer, *Warpaths: The Politics of Partition,* 210.
20. Susan Woodward, "America's Bosnia Policy: The Work Ahead," (Washington, DC: Brookings Policy Brief No. 2, May 1996).
21. United States Department of Defense transcript: Joint Press Conference August 5, 1997, Coalition Press Information Centre, Holiday Inn, Sarajevo. Available from: gopher://marvin.nc3a.nato.int:70/00/yugomain/1997/sftr0508.97
22. Department of State Bureau of Public Affairs, "White House Fact Sheet: Training and Equipping the Bosnian Federation," July 9, 1996. Derived from the temporary site http://www.state.gov/www/current/bosnia/bosnia_fs_training_jul9.html
23. Department of State Bureau of Public Affairs, "Albright Says U.S. Aid Tied to Efforts to Rebuild Multiethnic Society," Secretary of State Balkan Tour, June 3, 1997. Derived from the temporary site http://www.usia.gov/regional/eur/bosnia/sarajevo.htm
24. Susan Woodward, "America's Bosnia Policy: The Work Ahead," (Washington, DC: Brookings Policy Brief No. 2, May 1996).
25. United States Information Agency, "Serb Public Thinks Kosovo is an Internal Affair," *Opinion Analysis,* (Washington, DC: Office of Research and Media Reaction, 23 March 1998) USIA. This poll reports findings from a USIA-commissioned personal interview survey in Serbia, excluding Kosovo.

INDEX